This Quest For That
Final Horizon

Derrick La Saga

Heartfelt Thanks To:

To my loving, kind and eternally patient wife, *Lynn*. I never knew what it meant to truly know myself until you showed me how to live and be alive while doing it. I am so grateful for your love and support.

William, Jage, James, John, Melissa and *Calvin*. You were my family through high school and beyond; We were there for each other...... I never would have made it through without any of you. So thank you. With every bit of love in me, Thank You.

Richard Van Camp, David Malcolm, Jonathan, Judith and *Jeremy*. Thank you for the time, effort and support you showed me, it gave me that boost to continue through the last extra mile and see this dream come to fruition.

A huge thanks my Mother, Father and brother Christian because this book would never have come into being had it not been for the life you gave me.

My loving Father in Heaven. You have helped me through so much and have filled my life with huge blessings. There is a lot to you I do not understand but I do know you have my back if I just have Faith.

About the Author,

Derrick currently lives in Yellowknife, Northwest Territories. Moving there in Spring of 2010 for a job as an Electrical Apprentice, he later decided to switch over to the transportation profession in which he is currently a local fuel hauler. He met his wife, Lynn, there late in the fall of his first year north for which he is very happy.

His very first dream in life was to write a book. In high school there were many thoughts scribbled on desks, for which he was later told to wash away. One day a teacher asked why he didn't keep them in an exercise since they seemed good and creative. That was not the moment this dream began... but it was the moment in which Derrick's faith in accomplishing it did.

Foreword

I remember feeling very left out of the circle when I was growing up. Somewhere inside me I felt as though it was all backwards; that everything and everyone around me while seeming and appearing to be one way, was in reality, the opposite. Underneath it all it seemed to me that my friends were really enemies and enemies friends, that I was not being told the truth and there was some higher authority that was conducting this experiment to see just how many illusions I could take on and still retain a sense or knowledge of reality beyond it all.

The blank page became my best friend; I felt as though I could tell it anything and it would remember, exactly word for word as I put it, what I had confided. If I didn't want anyone else to know what I was saying, it wouldn't tell anyone. I found a beautiful place between the lines where I could run and run towards that hill where this ominous experiment was being conducted and no one could get in there to stop me.

Not all of the entries in this book are poems; there are also prose, songs and a few entries that are just random thoughts written down. There are three, three piece sequels that are, in terms of format, between poem and prose. While a large number of thoughts and topics are expressed throughout this collection ranging from *wishing to salvage a friendship* to *keeping busy in order to escape the things on one's own conscience* there is, however, a common theme. The desire to reach the other person, the last deepest truth, the ground on which we lay our foundation..... This quest for that final horizon.

This Quest For That Final Horizon

Contents:

Is It Innocence?

To me, one of the things my writing illustrates is the search for innocence. We all had it at one point in our lives regardless of how it may have been abused, overlooked or unappreciated. Once we lose it (no matter how long or terribly short we've had it) our focus becomes setting out to find that free, innocent, respected feeling once more. Some search endlessly, without relent or surrender and eventually the fear of slowing down becomes more important to them than finding it. That's when you know things must change, whether it's where you live, who you associate with or even just your way of thinking (which is almost always the best way). My search has been long, hard, and exhausting, and after so many miles, headaches from thinking about the mysteries of life, God, and the eternal void of space, I am finding that the way I think must change or my desire will be too hot and burn away my only hope for salvation, and it will become overlooked.

One time something hit and it hit me hard. I thought to myself that some want freedom while others want boundaries around them. This made me take a look at myself and ask, "What does this thought say? Does Wanting freedom mean wanting to be a leader and wanting boundaries around oneself mean wanting to be a follower? Or is it saying that wanting freedom means wanting to search for equal love; someone who can help bring back that innocent feeling and wanting restrictions is wanting to forget that feeling which you don't think you can get back?" There's always a reason for what you want. The healthiest place lies between being a leader and being a follower, between freedom and restrictions. Now ask yourself, do you agree with this? Well, I do. Many people care more about what they are searching for than they do about one another. The easier things are, the less distracted we are in our search for what we have lost, the better off we think we are. But look to the past and consider that those who have gone the farthest in their search for innocence are those who faced the biggest battles.

We have to realize that the search for innocence is not something that can be done alone or through other people. Do you remember how it felt? Don't just smile with those beautiful eyes of yours; take a moment and stir up imagery in your wonderful mind. Being unable to do it on your own doesn't mean you're not strong enough, clever or smart enough but because it's something you can only find with someone. Because it took two to create you so now it will take two to maintain you. It will take mutual love.

So search for that love. Search for it in the lowest gutters and alleyways, search for it in the highest clouds, but don't forget to search for it where it matters the most. In the places that make you feel innocent, free and respected.

To the Men of the Sea

Men with minds of stone,
are forever gleefully thrown,
into the moving horizon.
With nets of fish,
for a family's dish;
it will always be set (as taught).

Into times of hate, a cowards escape.
Out of times of prosperity; the brave ones charity,
all look upon the sea.

In times of madness full of sadness,
oh how the sea is no escape.
So pity the cowards and praise the brave,
for they both somehow endure that place.

Blind Image

So attached to your precious little sphere,
blind image to mend your fear.
Pity all that beat you down,
with time we know they'll break your crown.

And die forever,
why love to sever all that you are,
how could anything be far... in you!?
You wine and dine to feel second rate,
to all of the faceless figures that you hate.
Self-indulge in your lovely lies,
when all is over you'll wither and die.
All that you are, how could anything be far...?

You pound and toss upon this earth,
all the meaningless legions of yourself worth.
Can never seem to understand,
that your big empty castles made from sand.
Pity when the wind blows,
You'll cry and die forever,
so why love to sever all that you are,
how could anything be far... in you?

Empty Wings

So busy trying to fit sense to it all,
oh how many times did it all start to fall?
Getting to that point where it's all left to you,
leave this place behind to find my truth.

You were so busy trying to change your pain,
every time we'd always end up the same.
Now this game lingers on and on,
and I can't possibly change what's wrong.

Every time I'm alone I find another memory to ride,
Now as I look within I realize there's
Nothing left inside.
So I run and run from all that's done,
counting all those battles lost and won.

You never tried to figure me out,
every time I'd get close you'd find another route.
Now as I grow so tired of this race,
I begin to fear my hatred for this place.

Too much time with such small thoughts,
I was never really one for connecting the dots.
So busy leading myself astray,
my confessions go unread.

I'm just another addition to your hollow glory,
never given time to tell my story.
Because every time I cry... away you fly.
And I am left standing here never asked or told.

Box Under Tap
(Water Over the Top)

Nothing ever keeps its way,
although there never was a place to stay.
I take a look at you, seeing things so transparently.
I fight me and cave so emptily.

Now I'm just another lock,
box under tap, water over the top.
You pick the me I used to see,
now I'll be invading along with your foreigners.

You pause for the pressure that you love,
for me it's too much never enough.
Try to see why I run it through.
Tell you fake copies just never do.

Now I'm just another face, memories under fire
gunned down by hallow grace.
Now I'll be invading along with your foreigners.

Got to find another way to play your game,
because unanswered lies always end in shame.
I'm fleeing your memory a bitter forever,
all I can do is remarkably endeavour.

The Paper Pens Forcible Sin

Through all of the wind, under such rain,
my mind so distant from all of the pain.
I try so hard to crash so often,
cursed with this wretched love of failure.

Never left there (it's all too rare),
shackled to here (away is too painfully clear).
I cry to die but always end up with this desire to fly...
High in the depths.

Tell me, a tree to a tree, difference?
Change a mask into a cover, defeating victory.
The world laughs at your dark race and
how you left that mark with the paper pen.

Now gaze upon innocence,
so bright in its fight against the worthless treasures.
Kill the heartless love which keeps you in this prison of want.

Maybe your idea of born in sin,
is the cause for that sinister grin,
that you regretfully love so much.
Beat upon this place your crippling of unity,
and accept the strength of diversity.

My chains are slain,
oh how I did provoke until they began to choke.
Now I'm free to see your existence as a bitter joke.
Laugh away the glint in these eyes,
using it to shatter away your addiction to fly
in your tormented emotional caves.

Sure sense has never shown its face,
But show me who has perfect selfless grace.
Defend all legions within your region,
then upon your defeat, witness your empty strength.
Now, enjoying your self-betraying foreign grin,
you have enjoyed a look at forcible sin.

Chains of Reason

Frees himself from those chains made of reason.
Thinking his life to the knife, never any difference.
Somewhere he rests his head on a pillow made of grass,
wondering to the world how he'll ever last.

Never ever connects to anything yeah,
waits for the world to pull that string.
Run, run, run away.
Building the perfect little way, away from you.

Chasing down another restless hour,
through the flowers he finds himself crushed.
Discarding from hand a token of love.

Trying with so much might,
to get a glimpse of such a fright.
To get his heart going,
these days he finds himself slowing,
oooo-whoaaa.

Defeating Victory

I never tried to lie,
but instead fly with you.
Words of wisdom,
places of peace.
It was always just too few.

I was always running away from the world,
because I felt there was nothing for me to gain.
But I finally did give in though,
so I could be there with my pain
(because I had nothing but constant loss).

Nothing is ever over,
just like nothing ever starts.
And as I stand here and scream, "Where is my world now?"
I turn full circle to see that I've lost touch
of all my precious heart.

So I withdraw to see all the wondrous treasures I may never hold,
wondering to myself all their stories told.
Finding me outside all your pain and love.
I tell all the world, oh... how I've had enough.

Unlike All of It

Running all of you through my mind,
seeing your faces is all too kind.
Never really knowing if I knew you at all,
so I'll flee the world and await your call.

Because you seem too far away to be alone,
While I'm lost in this self-sentenced place to
unwillingly roam.
Seeing the worthless world and all its greed.
Never having anything is all you need.

New faces full of disgrace,
old people with their steeple.
Those of us that are neither here or there.
Bitterly realizing you're everywhere...and none.
Falling to the bottom, again your prize is the same.
As the loser has won another race (to be finished first).

Every time those links attach to the brink of insanity,
and every time I'm left with your unanswered Christianity.
Never ever told or shown why,
left in this box to slowly live while I die.

So I break your hold and wish to fly straight through your eyes,
soaring high in familiar skies.
I've always pursued where your unlike all of it,
but at times... it's all too tightly sewn.

I'll never die for any of you,
watch you smother all that is true.
And once you lay to collect your strength,
it will be known that you wasted it entirely.

I Will Fight (For You)

I feel alright all night.
Ain't nothing going to keep me down,
because I'm too alive to go around,
wearing your frown.
I'm too free to be your slave,
working through tears all for an empty grave,
I'll stand to see it all,
and when it's time to come down,
oh I'll fall...

And feel alright,
all night.
Just watch me take my flight.
Through all of the useless sorrow,
I will fight straight to you.

Because your all I knew.
I felt so alone,
like a dog without a home.
I would sit and let go of time,
but now I realize that's such a crime.

Oh baby,
you and me,
we will be free.
This love I could never deny,
take my hand now and fly with me.

Through Everything That is You

Through everything that is you
nothing ever seemed true,
and upon each escaping day
you're were desperate to find your way.

Never running through the bitter night,
proud to stand against it all and fight.
As you faced all the people of greed,
True humbleness is all you'll ever need.

Everyone stumbles from that race,
oh how they lift their heads and see
they've lost their place.
Now as the tears role down,
you got up and still followed his
glorious crown.

Always looking to the sky,
sadly wondering why,
they were never there for you,
even through all that you do.

But you know now you were seeing all
fake things true.
Within yourself it can been seen,
how you would never let yourself be free...
So the secret is known now.

Through everything that is you,
you know all that is true,
and upon each embracing day,
you continue on your newfound way.

Yesterday

Yesterday holds more reality for me than today,
so I sit atop it all and run these thoughts through my mind.

I never could see you anywhere,
so busy fitting me into you.
Fleeing through those thorns inside,
I would fall and see your stride and hate it,
because I felt it was always so fake.

Holding the honour that was your broken treasure,
to the sea you'd cast the coins of memories.
It became so rich with empty wealth,
and I was left to stand between your honour and duty.

There was everything there!
Time to put on the masks,
places to lie in them.
Oh, how they covered everything,
and left it all so warm with disgust.

All the rooms of my mind,
joining together to fit it wonderfully.
Never did show itself to the world,
for I was the pain I held;
tired so many times of me and you.

They are here now ready to be broken,
searching always for just a sight.
Places and meanings left the nothing I stumble under.
Here my eyes turn to the past with such eager opposition.

I search for them endlessly and die.
Left here to see the truth of it all,
you were never here or there
you were forever in no man's land.

So I rise to the beat of your drum,
shackled to the entire void defined with no choice to run,

and fall as it all caves from under me.

Now ambition-less upon this palace floor,
on my back the ceiling appears to be an endless journey away.
Those light fixtures, they sway with such careless ease.
And as I reach out to sooth the emptiness,
by covering them from sight with my palm,
to give myself a sense of fulfilment,
away they shatter.

And I am left... torn with their broken pieces,
blinded by the present light that never fades or goes away,
how many years shall it be another day?

Honourable Betrayal

Eyes see through you,
catching jealous lies,
just let it rest to listen,
understand, oh understand their view.

Never create and complain,
from the God's eye view.
Could never see it through.
Those hands tremble so,
to trust others with life's knife... never could!

Pick it up, dust it off,
keep it now and tell me.
Oh tell me, it's not too heavy,
beware for it slips and cuts the truth.
Save your breath, I know you don't have the strength.

You're causing this empty space inside,
and I just don't know what's left.
Honourable betrayal or empty meaning memories.
Just forget all of it, throw them away.
I've got this picture and it needs a bigger frame,
leave now because you're just too small to fit.

Prescription Destruction

Beneath the treasured moon, stars and sparkling sky
you finally spoke to me.
After all I had said to you (face now red);
after all the begging I gave to you.
"Don't think so much," was whispered.
Got through to you and this is what you say?
I never got through,
this is what I can see…
well this is what I say:

You want me more like you…
To never really care, gaze upon the wonders of nature,
or map out and tour the labyrinth that is my mind.
But that's not me, I need to pick things apart,
and piece back together to know what's really there,
and how it works for me.

Moonlight, show tonight,
the truth that has been long buried here.
From my closet door at night I see that total black,
spill out and possessively fill my room with fear and loneliness.
All these things I see in you,
all these things you gave to me.

My mouth is soare from telling you,
I wish not to see what is before your lingering eyes
dear father; they're filled with apathetic lust.
Hover about and ask for your daily dose,
can't give you any more prescription drugs,
maybe you should rest in your bed,
yeah take yourself to bed.
Sleep these thoughts away,
and I'll just drift out of here,
onto the streets where my rivers run.

Here I tread alone God knows,
barren land to the horizon.
Searching always in distant places,

running from their lying faces.
Tell me there's a road away,
wait...forget I just asked,
forgot all you do is keep me here.
Yeah, now we all understand,
why it's so hard for me to settle.
So many things you've kept everywhere,
eyes so blind and filled with lies.
I think this sword will now meet its place in the dust,
As where these feet stand is far from yours defend.

The Place They Call Here

So young with so much fun,
every day I'd sit under the watch of your gun.
Just looking at you seeing nothing at all,
now I realize you wanted to fall.

To keep down all that was true,
I knew you felt all I could do,
Oh, how I gave away all that I had,
just so I could see a reason to add hope!

I never could understand why,
you'd always rather cry than fly.
Away from the place they call here,
poor little girl lives in a tear,
don't die under the fear of knowing your truth.

So lonely with nowhere to go,
so humble with nothing to show,
sold everything for this place,
now you feel like such a disgrace.

Nothing ever seemed real,
you sit alone within its seal,
remembering when that time was ahead,
now you live eagerly fearing death is looming
above your head.

Up you rise to unwillingly fight,
I stand outside robbed of right.
Grasping my soul and locking it in.
Laying here now, I guess I'm just another empty sin.

You flee this place regretting it all;
I'm just sitting here waiting your call.
Never trying to show the love,
thinking this prison is more than enough.

I never wanted anything you said you'd give,

All I need is reason to live.
To fly away from the place they call here,
so I can rid myself of this dark, wet fear.

Time: The Bitter Stealth

To the minds of the many,
whose worlds are contained,
within a single empty achievement.
Never moving past their failure,
so they see their worlds through it.

Looking for the dark sky
the masses...they just stare with that eager eye.
The star that hangs above us all,
and your fate lies forever with all that you hate.

The places we avoid always seem to hold the key.
Oh to discard the remains of that mystery but
Somewhere in it lays truth for me.
It mightn't fit for any door though
for we once desired no more and beat them open.
Now that glow shines through not understood, just stolen.
So we leave it swollen and bleeding with thought.

Tell me your hidden vision,
show that unreachable glow your decision.
Discard everything that you see,
for what price will you be free?

The boundaries of all things eternal.
The death of everything that never sees life.
Empty voids of the rich,
and countless treasures of the poor.
It exposes the sight and blindness of us all.
But to time... all that is real is bitter stealth.

Apathy

Wanted so bad yet wished away,
here I remain standing alone not knowing which way to turn.
So many places where you could leave your trust,
so many faces that we love for lust.

I could never leave you with that,
because all I need is your everything,
and what I hold for you is anything.
Heavy air breath is a friend to me,
and heavy air breath will set me free.

Too many things all the same,
hate to think that you'd ever change.
So many people slowly turning strange,
don't know where this place is now.

I can't see you as this search is in the dark,
without my eyes I'm an easy mark.
Could you accomplish them for this blind man?

Through all the things that have held me down,
in the water you'd never see me drown.
Pulled to your shore I can't break free from your pride.

Clockwork Impressions

Clockwork impressions,
oh how that iron stings.
Standing there for your presence,
never left a thing.

Looking forward to the long gone past,
one-track mind in a runaway reason
and I fear it's uttered why.

Little sail boats far on the horizon.
Wanted its release but it was set free too soon,
all torn open and sewn up again,
now I've left the puzzle inside.

Turn way that look you give me,
you can figure it out simply,
I've killed the rat that eats the cheese,
no rodent left to hunt
now say you still need me.

Unaging hands hold you there,
tell me that light is not your guide.
It's all my definition of those expectations.
See they bind you but they do not define you.

You've lost it now so throw it all away.
Please see that your life is just another day and
don't finish rectifying that trap you set;
What's keeping you hear?
Such an absence of new and unexplored territory,
unbind your wings, fly, kill your fear.

Clockwork impressions,
oh how that iron stings.
All torn open and sewn up again,
have killed that rat and retrieved that eaten cheese,
give it to you; you've lost it now so throw it all to the wind.
Please take me away from the life that's just another day.

Outside Those Walls

Lost my meaning one time,
never saw it slip away.
Knew where it was though,
so I said I'd stay.

Breaking free from the fall,
hit the ground and I'm surrounded.
Little tunnel you once dug so I crawl;
out the other side I go happy with
what I found because I know.

I'll be outside those walls,
never gonna be one of those puppet dolls of pain,
where life is the game of catching drops of rain.
I've stood there with oceans and refused to drown.

Now I'm freely away,
able to safely say,
all that you left me with is a river
that I had to steal but it flows where I go,
wandering soul.

Now I'm searching for a reason,
trying to find a feeling,
looking for my eyes without I'm rendered.

So back I go,
don't like the walk,
but I enjoy the talk.
Defender of sanity,
too bad I'm never sane.

Now I'm seeing you for me,
all open for you to see.
Cold hard knife,
blood coloured life.

Nothing is for Nothing

What was it all for? I've learned where it all goes
so I'll wander to its resting place.
Give it up, I know there's nothing behind that face.

Cut the tongue that stirs the hope,
that I won't end up here again.
Maybe I'll return with the friend,
that I once took with me to find.

Rush the people that fill your time,
make them your pictures perfect pills.
They'll be just as you order them,
pay now and you'll still be too busy to swallow.

Gaze out the window that is afar,
enjoy the view behind the reflections,
of all the people that have made you who you are,
and just as this view is your cause... it's a dreadful curse as well.

Claim now to choose another as these are
gathered; the worthless for the sake of yours.
Retrieve it from that selection made.
No reason to bother, it's all as worthless as you.

What is this for? Show me where it goes,
reveal your one-way ticket ride,
I've nothing left inside for another tumble down deep.
I'll just lay here wondering if,
the strong man breaks or keeps way.
But for sure he's a user and breaks,
now watch his start, which fate will he turn?

Dig that up, to bury this deep.
No more than one hole for those feet.
Maybe there is no direction but it is not for nothing,
need to stop now to see nothing is for nothing.

Worthless Gold (Fools find)

I don't want anything that was taken away,
to want the stolen would be honouring the worthless.
A man can never be robbed of what he most treasures,
for I am yet to discover what it is I honour about my mirror image.

If you honour a worthless world,
then you will be bound to it.
If you tread on beaten ground,
you'll be a wandering eyepiece but no mind piece.
And if you believe that being unreachable in that secret place of yours is honour,
then maybe you should hold something worth protecting,
like honest dignity rather than illusion and resistance.

And I know what I honour is yet to be found,
for these wolves are treading the paths nightly.
Their teeth have torn trails in me,
but not before they stole my riches.
Theirs is larger wealth now; oh worthless wealth.

I long for nothing anymore,
only need a way out.
Feel the grin of untamed teeth.
Dry the blood before you run dry,
now grab the enraged beast but don't beat or eat,
the flesh that is a taste of your soul.

Pointless Knife

I steal everything I earn am I a thief?
Blew away all my words with a single breath.
Walking through crowds that never move;
seems to me nothing ever grows old and
now I'll remember what was told.

Never aged a day with life,
that rose left it all torn up and bleeding.
Look for it now as time wastes,
somehow it's all so pointless,
like candies without taste.

Nothing here to find please be kind,
tell me you know these words.
With or without understanding flow away
and I'll ask where have you've gone?
vanish every time I say no?

It's all like a pointless knife,
one slip and you bleed,
all over the floor, wait there's more.
It's alright if you weep every time you look,
but if it starts to hurt then let it spill.

Orange Covered Shapes

Bored, I'm bored,
so what do you want? I'll leave it up to you,
anything is fine with me,
everything is the same.

Wander your lonely walk for a meaning,
wander it so obediently for your lifetime.
Throw away the worry of running out
since this one is all there's left.

So blind from watching an empty sky,
so beautiful when you give a shove to
jump start the march to everywhere we've already been,
places we hate like never before.

Too busy thinking to speak,
with you I toss these confessions into the light,
your too busy listening to understand what they mean.
So I'll just leave emptier.
Damn your impossible cover of tears,
as it drowns out the light you've spilt
but not before it burns to cinders all that you love.
Learn when to close your eyes and open your heart.

Terrible amounts of words everywhere,
so many you've no chance to really care,
reading on I grow to hate each one,
conceived with lies to the fire it flies.

I could hate without a single thought,
as you admire those orange covered shapes,
just like me but why would I?
My friend, sure you can love what I do too!
We would be brought together,
no longer lonely,
come now, gaze skyward with me.

Original Sin

So long, inner child,
it was nice to know I had a little youth left.
Memories dwell within of all the places you took me to show,
But now there's nowhere left for us to go.

Oh good bye, dear sweet boy,
it was nice to know I was still young.
All the playgrounds you led me to
but there's nothing left for me to do.

So I'll say so long momma,
and may you find your original sin,
all the tears over all the years,
yet you never felt a thing.

A heart so big and eyes so bright,
I just know you've got the strength to fight.
Pick up your sword and leave your mark,
the scar runs from my head to my heart,
and we both know that's where you'll be.

Enemy in the mirror

Everything unknown fills your head,
all that you live for only renders you dead.
So where is it you want to go?
What keeps you moving?

Is there enough to make you see
that you'll never beat me.
Your headed just past the limits,
always further than the distance
which goes on forever so can you endeavour?

What keeps you going?
Is there enough to make you see
that you'll never catch me?
Run and you run until you end up here,
right where you started then you discover,
the fear that you flee is me,
the one who stares back at you from the mirror.

Quiet Place (Still Desire)

Climb a tree, pick a leaf,
let it shade you from the light.
Now take a look,
I'm down by the brook,
Won't you come ride the current with me?

Where are we going? You ask.
Here, let me paint it on your heart,
rolling meadows of oh so sweet release,
offer a stillness we can use to start.

Don't you know it comes as you go along?
Look within, I've left it there forever,
careful detail of my heart and soul.

Now look at me and cry,
I thirst for your love.
There is no fear for I know you're pure.

Look at the water,
see my face so clearly under.
Watch the fish swim,
jump on in and drift away from the world with me.

Unreachable Focus

The autumn breeze soars its way through the skyward trees,
hear the rustling of leaves as they all blow away.
Before my feet they land and wilt and then hits
the amazement; I just can't see how I would be their destination.

I take yet another step,
beneath my feet I crush them without remorse.
This leaves me asking, "Should I gather and preserve them?
Even though their time is past now?"
Oh, it's as clear as the buried, tangled roots of these giants.

Now I feel the coolness of the wind,
such a saviour on a day like this.
I pocket my hands in this long, furry coat of mine,
maybe I'm so cold because I guard myself from the wind.

Am I as blind as all of this?
Remorse seems to be my only course.
Perhaps it would all just disappear if the shadows
that haunt me would cover themselves with the colours of life.

Dying now as I'm so drained and grey,
thinking things never go my way.
Billions of thoughts swirl around me
Do they all point to a purpose?

Purple Paint

Invisible to the masses,
just keep on walking by,
lay here in a tear of purple paint,
so pleasantly thick I can't breathe.

I answer you,
I'm too busy thinking to speak,
then I must have the words to say,
not yet, but it wouldn't change those thoughts
of yours anyway.

Self-imprisoned in your eyes,
does that make me your enemy?
To some, Mr. sun casts shadows,
but to others, it merely exposes.

So swear my name in vain,
all I'll do is watch them break.
Purple paint oozes out in spots,
fury flies with clenched fists,
splatter on the floor, as my body and face hits it,
dazed and smothered gasping for breath.

Hazy and almost black, there's no sight for me,
but I won't die, since I now you won't get far
with my name.

The People

Fire lights up an icy sky.
All the people stand around wondering why as it slips away;
can't you see it doesn't mean a thing!?

Complexity seems to be,
the very fabric of these childhood streets.
All my thoughts are leaking;
all the people are speaking,
of just how far I've gone astray
now that I've finally found my way.

Wind so cold keeps me so high.
Its purpose useless now,
as I glide above and beyond the flames of the desert
for no longer am I deserted!
I'll fly past it all with no more memory
and meet you there just like I did;
when we were among the people.

I see your face full of contempt,
you spot me and frame mine through the barrel of a gun.
My smile kisses the bullet that you leave for me.
So now as I lay here so guilty conscious free
my unblinking eyes watch the red river run so long and dry.

Journey

Rest your face upon the pillow,
hear a repetitive sound in your head.
A dream where a man trudges through a blizzard,
disturbs your sleep and recalls everything she said.

Always searching for the place,
the place where everything is reverse.
I hear all they say,
so how is it that I'm still so far away?

Friends are foes so bitter,
and likewise as well, how so?
Like a confession, this goal,
or is it all in my isolated mind?

Through trees so tall,
under sky so free,
I look ahead so ambitiously,
and finally reach this place.

So far ahead the sites,
not a single soul to find!
I don't know where I came from,
and don't know where I am going,
as the rain washes away all I seem to remember.

It always feels the same as you,
no matter what I do these lies will always be true.
Oh if only I know why I want to die,
I might know where to go to change.

So where would it go if I let it all slide?
And where would I hurt if all these things I choose to hide?
Now I repeat within myself:
fill all empty heads
honour all ambitious eyes,
chase all foolish dreams,
and live in soothing lies.

Pillow

Too much writing lately leads me to suspect I hate to hold.
Why do I sing it all? Do you think you could tell me?

That last one ran wild, didn't it?
So long I can't remember it all.
Now go back and read it,
will that make it any clearer?

I try to deceive you but that's a laughing joke.
Such a coincidence to have met like this as
The curtains torn away and
the light casting so many shadows…
do your eyes sting and chest pound through the
fire?

No, I didn't mean them to!
Okay I'll just go and walk the streets,
the sacred little groove between the lines.
Run and walk along the way,
race the lead as it dies,
poor pity for that one,
but I'm still here with you.

Hold the body of flesh,
feel his heart through the tears.
A flood of shame new for all the times I was wrong,
but you taught me not to feel bad,
so much as fortunate for your love.

And I don't feel foolish anymore,
nor do I say "Whatever"
to myself when I think of all the times I hurt,
instead I try to deal with them.

You help as you hold my head, soothing it, catching my tears,
absorbing them until you're so wet.
It seems this pillow of mine,
Is no longer as dry as myself.

Illusive Fairies

Fairies on the horizon,
never caught to decision
of where to go.

Let them open your mind,
hear the words of their voice;
Ask what you need.
Since your awareness won't let you know
of where you belong.

It's been a far trek
since I tried to figure out what I've needed.
Could you make it any clearer
by telling me what I'm confused about?

We can help you make it,
only if you don't fake it.
Let's go back to the start
through the painful hate.

Yeah the reasons clear;
now we see how deep this fear is in you.
With a glittering laugh they say,
"Keep yourself strong,
and wander your theory until you know it,
as well as you know where to find us."

Now I stand finally knowing it;
Silently tossed to and fro.
Fighting the waves as I pull closer,
And see courage to battle back against fear.

New Shadows

Common code of the worlds about,
so separated as they prey among the countless lights.
Don't know what they need from what they want,
when they pick their God of choice.

Steal away what doesn't mean a thing,
Have you offered what you've stolen yet?
I'm sure since it's danced and passed about,
Show case image a disgrace to the isolated original.

How can I forget the words that have silenced me?
Spoken oath in a jury of jealousy.
All meant well for the time I'm told.
Broken guidance lasts forever as time ticks down.

If you can't feel it; leave this place.
If you don't want it; don't make it your disgrace.
Break the chains that keep you free,
it's the only thing that binds and blinds.

Maybe I bring it on myself as away from them I step.
Make the move to go on… but where's a safehold now?

Drug Addiction

Dare the otherside of the wall,
feel the pull as you slide and fall.
Follow the frequent path,
good-byes fill my head when I don't look,
but only when I don't.

Tidal waves form against the future,
bridges cast this shadow over my flowing questions.
Swim the endless canyon in one last race and
see them in arms on the otherside searching for my face.

When will these wings fly away?
Another day thinking I can go there.
It's all the fictional part of my mind,
so why do I care so much?
Why do I care so much for what can kill me so fast?

Unnecessary poison for the mind,
forget all the faces when you reach that free place.
Know these things run you by the long way, all day.
I feel it again and understand the answer...
I want it again! It's my beloved cancer.

To Know

What spurs in you,
only dies away to come once more renewed.
It's never that transparent
but the view you want is clear.
Now can you get it?

This stillness pulls me under,
movement in my mind keeps me alive.
Where should I give the go?
These things are all I know.

Empty liars give their word,
You'd leave them all to die.
But you know they'd give it all to fall to you.
Because we all want humbleness that hides the pain,
but there's nothing here to use as a cover.
And yet we remain, oh we remain the same as one another.

Now I find myself thinking,
this stillness pulls me under and keeps me alive.
Now where should I give the go?
These things are all I know.
So what have I to show?

Gentle Ambition

My children are these words,
their sins I deserve.
Some things are better left unspoken,
sometimes you wish to be broken
to be stronger at the mending.

And everyone wants it from inside,
to give it all away from yourself, oh what a pride!
Then when they don't understand what you see,
the darkness falls once more and your defiance is your guide.

I don't believe you know the mystery you long for.
I don't believe you understand the part of the mystery you live and die for.
These things I could never accept,
since your drive was to know why you kept going.

Reason, it doesn't solely lay in the glory of perseverance.
Reason, it doesn't survive entirely from the feelings for another.
Reason, it's never mistaken for your longing for fulfilment.
Reason, it can't be defined as opposition.
So where can we find this reason of yours?
Or has is run its course? Has it led you astray?

Fading away are today's sunset clouds as they
Are putting to rest all these things I ponder.
And this moment of peace gives a taste of a mindset I fear to desire.

The Trees' Duty

The wind through the trees,
sooths my soul with its melody,
leaves of countless colours,
fly before my eyes.

High in the sky they flutter
before the invisible force
blows them to the road to rest-
I want to do the same!

I lay here in the scattered shade
thinking I stand out well enough
to cast an uncut shadow
between me and the million alike.
Where no difference can be seen.

A boy walks along and spits upon a leaf.
Up to it I go and pick it up to feel,
it's cold, slimy texture and I think of how it was dry,
and vibrant before it was cast aside.

Warrior's Cry

Brutality in the hands of honesty sheds the blood of a warrior strong.
None of them can survive yet none of them want to die so the battle rages on.
Fighting the truth never makes you a lie but when you turn your back from resolve,
Everything you've bled for runs down your face and makes you a failing disgrace.

March through fields of disease welcoming the sickness with every step.
Run through walls of fire feeling your skin melt as you prove your desire.
Fight in all the meaningless battles with pride, without a single second thought.
Because without momentum; you couldn't be kept going here.

Rivers of blood through fields of bones,
their souls now run with the current all alone.
So many faces in one small place and they still can't see one another.

The Frustration of Heartache

My head pounds at my hearts rapid sound,
and the emptiness there is such an ache.
You think I want it all about me,
but I don't care who I am or happen to be.

Now doesn't this make you feel so much stronger,
I can see how you're that much different.
None of this matters much in real life;
all blood is shed the same with a knife.

Take a loss with brisk full strides;
Walking along the wall submerged within.
In your head it runs so wild,
just like you want it in real life.
All blood is shed the same with a knife.

Let loose, smash the tv.
Grab the glass, right through the window it goes,
hit them once or twice as you wonder why,
all these urges rise and fall within you,
so why not continue, as the distantly free man?

Dark Breeze

Under and away from the sun,
I have my shady protection,
as I lay in the shadows of the trees.

The people, they play before me,
games I love so much.
Ask me to be a part of it but
I decline, no worries for the rest.

Right now, I have what I know before me,
memories of happy days, oh happy they're here again.
My smile is good for you.
No matter where you go, is where I'll be.

Beautiful Garden of Jealousy

Children play, separately.
Games they know, need to be.
They're so distant when they hold my hand,
sit in silence with them and up it comes again.

I tell them "This is so strange to me.
One for everyone, I'm always left scraping mine out.
Takes you a mile yet I'm flying further!
Where I land, I walk along alone."

In that place, quick reminders are all but dead,
and golden sunsets ease what's said.
There's always purple flowers growing so fresh,
their sweet aroma helps me forget the mess.

All Over Again

So low I always lay,
my mind goes back to all those places again.
I can't handle this alone, oh my God I've lost my tone,
now I'll just drift away to die.

I won't read the first before writing the second.
I always keep it alive that way,
so perhaps I will follow the feeling this time.

One day my man destroyed a part of himself,
it was more than what you could see.
And to this day he longs to search for it,
yet he can't seem to find the will to move,
from the bliss in which he lives.

Why did you have to kill me?
Why did you have to take this from me?
Why can't I get past this?
Why can't I find my way?
And why will I go numb again...once I get this out?

Here I am dwelling again,
in the memory of a bittersweet mystery.
Where the answer forms all over again
whenever you begin to search for it.

Curiosity: The Adventurer

When it comes to mind,
it brings with it something more to find.
I wish I knew what is strange to me,
but all this time of wandering has set those things down.

I'm sunk in traveling thoughts,
contemplating what it was you brought.
This investigation I will solve
and I'll reach the vision I see.

Now there goes my mind
but I still have the focus.
Because I don't want to go without it anymore,
and I shouldn't have to think it over,
when it's what I have to hold.

So I will treasure it all for fun,
you can't catch me when I'm on the run!
Swollen feet upon the dirt they beat.
I anger the God of Earth,
who tosses me above the clouds.
Where I glide along with the wind;
clutching the wings of soaring falcons.

Keeping Sight

When the sun is out,
and the day is clear,
I'll find my way to you.

When the night falls
and the darkness magnifies the shadows;
I'll simply turn my head away
from the demons of my life
and follow you always.
Because you have the light that has guided me,
the strength that has protected me,
and the wisdom which has taught me everything I know.

Advice for a Mission

Whatever you give will be cherished most
if it's worthless in the physical.
Don't confuse yourself with the world,
don't take when you give.

Come on, with what I hand to you,
you know what to do with it.
You have an endless pouring tool this way,
the hope is rising now so believe!

Put your head clear in focus
to see your unstable progression
is your only confession.
I know there's a million different things you've seen.

Don't look to your left, nothing there.
Don't look to your right, just fight your way.
Keep yourself within your purpose,
And the world at bay.

Hatred Meets Defiance

I'll never see what's taking me,
so alone I endeavour this eternal suffocation.

The words you forbid from these lips
will be spoken to the world through my motions.
Your strength never seems to resist,
one day it will break, this is my notion.

I've found my hatred for the day,
greater than my passion for the setting sun.
Eyes from every corner staring at me so easily-
I see their souls burn in contempt.

Please scorch my fire alive,
take it to a new size.
Please burn my life from the inside out,
it's so much faster this way.
A lost less pain and you can say,
a giant you've set out to slay.

Searching in your Destination

Burn in the scorching brightness,
your hope swells as the tide goes low.
Upon this island you've been left alone,
it's so big now can you get away?

Unseen treasures grace your eyes,
in your head all those questions fly.
Wander a path in hope of new pastures.
break in two and nearly die,
When you realize searching alone is a disaster,
in this place of no escape.

Lay and listen to the birds tell you with their ringing cries,
that the beating of your heart; that still small voice inside
Is the force which has been calling you.
So come now and begin these feet upon the path within.

Submerged Gloryscreen

You push me to rejection,
within it I lay and collect my strength
and put the paces between us so high in number.
The distance here reaches your eyes,
as you lose sight of me over the horizon and into the sun.

I'm burning up all over,
black as the damp ashes of the flame,
that once burned for you.

Behind you I arise out of the uncertainty,
you don't turn but instead you remember me,
and how I used to be in sadness of that long gone day.

Over your head I pass bringing it all to its end.
Now aren't you watching that horizon still?
A beautiful sight before it lights up,
and you're suddenly reminded of why you come here again.

Your Own Stranger

Searching for a last escape,
falling within I can only hate.
No substance anywhere anymore.
Trapped in the barrier,
that you died to protect.

Hung myself with rotten rope,
used life's knife to cut that hope.
Nothing real to define my courage,
burned it all trying to discourage
the vision in your mirror.

And I could look to the sky,
maybe even wondering why,
they all smashed the glass
to forget the faces that where
strapped to me so they'd be free.

Now I just stare,
unable to care,
as I walk along your illusive path,
all the years in this treacherous wrath.
Asking, "Have you deceived me for a reason?"
Now I may be someone else it seems.

Rivers and Rabbits

Mountain tops overlook it all,
snowy lopes against the wind.
One more grasp then you pull,
far above the plateaus as their meanings
are gone now without a worry.

Beautiful forests of towering giants,
lush green carpet upon the earth,
rivers and rabbits running so wild,
a golden sunset across the horizon
sets it all aglow, let go, be free!
Now steady your grip as you climb for your heaven.

Swiftly through the curtain of green grass,
feel its texture of life as the river ripples.
Run to the water and follow its direction,
wet fur, beating heart, persistent strength,
wild beauty tamed in a sanctuary of peace.

In the eyes upon the slopes of the sky,
seeing the rabbit racing with the current.
Together they flee the peaks,
out of the forest, away from the shadows.
Upon the river rocks, feel their strength,
a creature of innocence keeps its pace,
even when the water is its obstacle.

Dizzying heights swirl about,
free fall from the skyward perch.
Onto, and into the carpet of the earth,
witness the strength of giants
tremble and break,
stain them with stinging blood,
as their shadows fall around you.

Sigh at the marks left as you taste the first,
Second one a lasting reason why,

as you follow his tracks.
Backwards now you go your way through the shadows.
Don't become lost just remember the details from your view.
You choose another direction.
Hey, hey, hey, hey, hey
Oh yeah, oh yeah.

Oh you want to catch me dear dreamer?
Didn't you see my swift pace along the river?
There grow some flowers which drip with aroma,
And their petals float with the wind.

Maybe they can help you
disappear for the surprise.
Sink low and shower on their roots
so they will put it all to a wicked disguise.

There's a bunch fluttering about,
Near the water's edge.
Oh, I think of where they will lead me,
As they are many as one.

From the roots of sweet smelling danger,
I suddenly meet them as you finally awake,
From the showers of covering love.

Trickles of purple pleasure wash off,
Aroma fading as my joy flutters away,
Now I'm dreaming I'm under the surface,
Embracing a kiss knowing for today I gave this.
As I'm lying and floating so relaxed and still.

Courage:
The Man in the Bright Light Moon

Don't want to go to that quite place again,
not while I think at least.
All these words echo the same-
especially when they come from there.
It's never any different,
yet so unrecognizable.

Can't you give those x-ray eyes a break?
You know exactly where it is!
Don't know it's what you're searching for though.
That I can be sure of.

Every single thought is just another distraction.
Every single moment is just another empty feeling lost.
Maybe if you collect your thoughts for a while,
you'd feel real enough to build that courage of yours.

And I've analysed it all so much,
these sights can be read in my definition.
Forever again you're so busy searching me,
that it's overlooked all over again.
How much more can I take?

How many more days until I forget my dreams,
I wake and he asks for nothing less than too much,
how can he feel like I owe something?

Amazing how it's passed to me,
all the things you left here just to see
how far it could be carried.
To the man in the bright light moon I gave a call,
down he came to catch my call, came to catch my fall.
Upon so many enchanted footsteps
he led me to this peak,
and I gazed upon that soothingly yellow horizon.

I cried a tear then for once,

Just an honest tear.
So astonishingly empty it seemed.
To show everything and return nothing,
What was it that the man spoke to me?
Surely the words will return? Oh yes,
he said to me in such honest truth:
It is your heart that will lead you,
It is your mind that will teach you,
It is your pain that will deceive you,
But it is your courage that will save you.

People of the Moon

Connect the separation,
in your eyes I see the desperation.
Try hard to understand my thoughts
But brainwaves wash it all away.

Your sufferings are here because of the tide,
comes in high when you're still down low.
From up off the rocks you dive,
ready to feel alive then away it flows
and you split your face.
Upon the rocks below so why go again?

Struggling to stop this cycle,
If you stand for a moment to watch,
How it all is, you'll see the reflection in the water.
It repels from you and merges into
sinking tar.
And so away from this shore your eyes turn
Because this becomes something
too much for you.

Loving the Hell

The shadow on the pave,
his soul I'd love to save.
But how do I know if he's not a void instead,
and how do I know if he isn't already dead?

My question is the expression on his face,
It's impossible to know why he'd come to this place.
From where I stand he seems to be a lot like me,
why can't you open your eyes to see?

The echoes of the whispers,
of the shadows,
of the people,
who stand away, they all stand away.
When I move for help they all run away...
Into the distance.

Guided Decision

My mind, it's locked away.
The direction I need to go,
I think I'll never know.
Scream and I'll hear you,
cry when you need me,
just guide me truthfully.

My voice is for the nearest ear,
my cry is for the deepest heart.
The truth is never really clear
and we're always far from the start
when we want to find it.

I'll tell you, I don't trust anyone.
They always point their guns;
you fire the bullets that scar my face.
I pull the bullet out and the bloody river runs.

From it you come and I realize my trust
is misplaced in you.
I go on stronger and more alone than before.

Bloody Water

Brick churches with cold, iron crucifixes,
wooden shacks where the richest dwell in poverty.
They both shine upon the road their dim lights,
which are not for my eyes, oh blind eyes to see.

Away from them I walk,
along the trail I talk to myself,
about how hopeless and vague it has been for me.

Carrying on until the nighthawk sings his song,
I stumble upon the jagged rocks;
torn and bruised it spills.
Staining the path this traveling bard has chosen.
Now they will know my secret travels for sure.

Oh, flow rapid red water current,
oh mix with the rain dear smotheringly thick blood.
Because I'd like them to see,
that you're both the same to me... liquid.

Laying in the darkness once again,
my feet they steal away.
Screams and moans are now helpless groans,
as I lay soaking in this bloody water bath.

The Flaw in Ambition

My thoughts no longer know this memory,
I no longer know me anymore.
Seems I've covered a thousand miles,
yet haven't moved a step.
Am I the one to blame?
Am I my own stranger?

So I look up once again
for a simple reason why,
and cry as I fail to find words that are you.
Now I see what's true,
they can talk, these words,
they can talk.
They confess, these words,
they confess.

To me this is what they say:
Take time with your wandering mind,
let it settle anywhere in air or on ground.
Even in the ocean to flow along with the waves.

Now follow in fear,
but be not fleeingly afraid.
Know it'll be clear and love that catch;
Your searching for yourself!

And I play this game way too much,
matching down words, it's become a crutch.
And I play the game way too deep,
spilling so much that I always weep.
These confessions I hate,
these confessions I cannot escape,
get them out to survive the day.
Lost them now, which path was my way?

Offering

I'm kind of crazy; I'm what I like to call
a self-conversationalist.
Over analytical about the smallest little joy,
blow it up till it carries me past the rain source,
it's all so good because it doesn't take anything for
me to see things come alive.

Please laugh, it's better than holding pain.
Don't bury me, okay... let's just walk in vain.

Who likes to smudge the daze?
Aren't things confusing enough as they are?
There's so much I plug into this,
that my occasional tears of fuel,
are set afire by this anger I hold.

The ashes I smudge add another shade.
Another mile added to the riddle.
As I hide from the scorching sun,
won't you sit with me instead of burning like you are?

I'll simply lead you to a place of revelation,
then you will feel the joy you never had.
Your eyes will see their beholder for the first time,
No longer will it all be captive at the hands of vanity.
Would you lead me to wherever you've never been?

Where Am I Today?

Deadly little lies,
bow your smothered head.
Don't even know why they come,
or know why they arise.

No... whatever,
keep it going,
where am I?

This place of mine is so broadcast,
should I keep it all in?
What does it matter anyway?
I will explode only to oppose,
this one here I chose.
So set off, set off... again.
Set off, set off... subside.

Swimming soothes the pain,
no I'd never drink.
Mangled branches scratch
a lonely twisted fate,
keep it strong!
Keep it going for today.

But none of this is real,
it's all just in my head,
death is cruel to me,
so I think I'll lose myself instead.

Crying Clown
(Fool's Fears)

Fall to the edge,
look on over think your down now,
but your only looking for a lover.

And I can see your very best friend,
is that part which helps you forget
what it is you most regret;
Because of all that is lost from memory.

Leave them all so far away,
stay here to watch them dance and sway.
Making a tear he feels it all wash down;
too many laugh at this lonely clown.

Narrow little door has been broken in before.
See the footsteps led astray,
lose those footsteps as you turn and continue on.
Not afraid of what's within.

Reason... is my illusion,
freedom is too much of a confusion.
Do you know where these ideas come from?
I think I know where they're made,
from the place where innocence died in its crusade.

Do you feel these walls caving in?
Worry not, nothing's as tall as that bluish gold sky,
and you feel like your trapped in this sin?
As you want to fly, why wait?
Change is closing in, you might not recognize it tomorrow,
stranger things have happened child.

These eyes are so bright,
can't they see it's all waiting for you?
So why not leave this all so far away?
Why remain here to simply dance and sway,
How much of you will drown in sad tears?

Swimming Bubbles Drift

Swimming bubbles drift,
see your thoughts shift.
It's all the same,
no one's to blame.

Feeling so much less,
needing that much more.
Tears of lust stain this dress,
through the water I soar.

Drowning as I drift under a lake,
eaten by the moths in sweet delight.
They never feel the fall,
notice me crawl,
or even hear me call!

Focus on the rapid eye,
see it settle on a worthless lie,
don't ever care for the stare,
see through you if you cry.

Lone wolf weather the storm,
weak and sick you carry on.
So how you gonna take it?
You got to make it,
just don't fake it.

Silent Voices Whisper

Silent voices,
defend my purpose,
its seems to me,
they're below the surface.
Are you lost?
With nowhere left to go in the light of day?
Are you lost?
Do you believe you can still find your way?

Oh, I've become lost again,
confusion consumes me.
Desire burns my flame,
as disarray leads the way.

I wander everywhere,
on this island of hatred.
It's all mine these lies,
in a pain that is sacred.

My silence speaks to me:
Only trust the truth with you,
and it is this that reveals me.
Now I burn under the sun.

Revealing all my shadows,
none left for me to use as refuge.
All those wicked eyes hunt for me,
as I'm left lying in the open.

The Face of Vengeance

Batter everything with meaning,
will that define your cause?
Jewels of gold you hold alone,
can't you see so many stand beside you?

Call out to the heroes of your land,
glorify their names with innocent blood.
Watch the red river run so long and dry,
march your way through innocent children as they die.
Feel the life surge as you take your drink,
demonic pride twists your bloody lips.

Stand on your throne and look down to see
how it's leaving them.
Understand that today children lay in the streets dying,
today another family perished as the bombs went flying.
Today screaming from the heavens,
birds from so called paradise kill the life of the land.

Oh but hold your worries,
your flag is still above the rest, honour your soldier as he falls.
This gives warmth to your evil heart.

Brimstone upon flesh, painful screams from the muddy dirt.
Watch a solid father burn and die,
is this good cause for your reason why?
Oh good God why?

Shame, Regret & Admiration

Burning a hole straight through my head,
Just standing there now wishing I was dead.
I go there to get away,
It's all over now, so what is there to say?

Believe the words will come,
even in the absence of faith.
Only live for the moments,
that will lead you away from disgrace.

Now look to the sky as you feel it again,
love them when they're everywhere.
Look to the sky as you're trapped again,
hate them when they're all that's there.

Now breathe the breath that has become cold hard death,
thinking too many things end the same.
Now feel the life escape the lips,
another moment that will end in shame.

I let all the thoughts of my mind run wild,
instead they all fall in line.
Feeling like a lost little child,
now I see they observe the ultimate design.
Smile (your face is pretty).

Silent Dog

Hear it play awhile,
helps you see tomorrow.
Why not stay awhile?
There's peace you can borrow.

Another moment gone,
do I believe they can be used?
So maybe I'm wasting as I wonder
or is time my crime?

Ride your kite and feel the dog bite as you crash so hard,
perhaps the wind will catch you next time.

Fight all night for a quiet moment,
bleed in need and cry out in silence.
Desire like fire; thinking I haven't really burned the flame.
Lost in a stillness with you instead is not the same.

I have the burned eyes and I yell the silent cry.
I need the question why because I want the answer to die
so I can make my own and fly so high.

Seasonal Food

Water spilt over the surface,
sitting in the chair he doesn't care anymore.
Lays his face on the table top
and follows the little river wherever it may lead.

Through the snowy fields, where he played so long ago,
through the houses, they're soggy now as the river goes.
Memories take his mind to a mystery he wishes to find which
has been lost in these blissful seasons;
lost with the progress of life.

Looking back to the river as it flows out of town,
He's riding it as it flows over the edge.
A waterfall for one and all until it hits the bottom.

Lifting his head,
he dries his tears and wipes their trail from the table,
sweeping the salt away,
he then picks up the slice of bread and tosses it into the dog dish.
Walking outside he looks upon
his town and says, "This isn't my town anymore."
Then walks back inside for another night.

A Boy and His Mom

I reveal myself to her,
but she still stands beside me.
Oh, I feel the warmth of her gift,
my morning coffee!

On my way to start my day,
the sun looks so bright in the sky.
I walk along and sing along with the birds,
the warmth of the coffee burns my hand as I let go.

To the ground it falls,
staining my clothes and I hear my
mothers calls:
"Come here my son,
I'll fix you up handsome for everyone,
and you will be the most beautiful boy!"

The Eyes of the Dark Knight

You see all the knights as they form their line,
you fear for your life as they see your crime.
you run from the day to hide in the night;
Tell us all now…will that stolen sword really help you fight?

COURAGEOUS THIEF!!
To steal and fight with such a grief!
He stands alone on the hill up there,
soon he'll run down and die without a care.

Marching down now he gives a swing,
defeating a dark, dark knight,
whose very last thought... is to finish the fight!
Delivering a massive blow,
to the ground they both fall and bleed,
the thief looks to the sky in tender need.

They all stand around and judge his soul,
he just lets go since he knows he'll be swallowed whole.
They ask, "What will you say with your final breath?"
In answer "Just pass down my blade in a cold hand of death."

Through his heart the blade did pierce,
and as he lay upon the earth his life ran fierce.
As they turn to leave him drift to sleep
their eyes foresee that he died long ago,
just like the rest.

Excuses for Nothing

Everything seems to be the same,
as he walks away in your mind.
Changes tear your life apart,
as every days a game.

You know winning is what you go for,
and you know winning is all you'd ever have to show.
You know winning is what you go for,
and you know winning is all you'd ever have to show.

So instead you keep in your place,
don't want only one thing to show.
If it's not every last piece of gold,
you'll turn your head and say "No,"

You know your spent and you know your bent,
and you know your spent and you know your bent.

Is winning the game
your life?
Is leaving them all behind
a thrill for you?
Is being alone with your reason
victory in your eyes?
Is being blind to the reason of
your pain soothing?

You want to be alone,
it's got to be how you see things.
So much easier when nothings in the way
of how you want your day for everyone.

What about you?
Won't you come have some lemonade?
"No, I like the beer!" you say,
"It kills the fear I have inside."

So again you drink,

and tilt that celebration of yours upside down.
So again you drink,
and tilt that relaxant of yours upside down.
So again you drink,
and tilt that excuse of yours upside down.
So again you drink,
and tilt that curse of yours upside down.

So don't turn me bottom up anymore,
I can't stand to be your blind eyes or mask.
I'm not here to be a window for you,
keeping your mind with me has become a task.

Monkey Morning

I break the stillness in the morning light,
I turn and look down to the earth, so far down.
Perhaps if I'd awake I could travel to friends,
but I've lost them in the dark lonely night.

The suns ray's shine upon my face,
my eye's burn so I look for a place to go,
out of the branches I fly with speed,
thirsty for water from the river banks.

Diving in for a swim,
refreshment hits me with awaking pleasure,
I reach the bottom and pull along the rocks,
and what is it that I see?

A golden fish, a tasty dish
some refreshment for my tummy,
a stick I pick, a jab and grab now I have my meal.

Out of the river I walk;
to the shore where I will eat.
Sitting there upon my rock with the water
dripping and running all over,
I suddenly remember a place to go.

Along the path I journey to Bob's house;
Anxious to share this meal,
and as I arrive, what is it that I see?
He also has a meal for me!

"Hello, friend, I see what you have"
"Put away for good times, that's what we did!" he exclaimed,
"And surely this is one of them."
"So let us eat," I say,
"Yes, let us rejoice together!"
And there we sit, eating our fish,
wrapping our wet fury tails together,
So happy and warm.

Shining Wish: From Recluse to Fulfilled: Pt. 1

That Moonlit Road
(Starring Matthew)

Walking along the street in the moonlight,
the rain gives the road a sparkle,
clouds drift along overhead,
as a cool midnight breeze rustles the road side grass.

With his long hair flowing down over his big black coat,
a steady pace he keeps back to his apartment,
hands in his pockets, eyes to the sky,
the shining stars are out in numbers.

While he walks, he thinks "It's been a waste, we did nothing at all.
Every time we start to connect, it all starts to fall apart,
what's so wrong with what I want?
I only want to fulfil it, to reach the other end!"

Crossing the road and hopping onto the sidewalk,
big black windows stare at him so blank.
The gentleness of the wind subsided to a howling rage,
as his coat is blown up around him,
his hair's sent everywhere and a chill runs up his spine.

Pushing his coat down with his right arm,
he pulls out the porch key with his left,
THUD, THUD, THUD, THUD....
Up the steps he walks and at the door he stops.

"Oh God, another night with the loneliness I dread." he thinks,
"I know what it is I want, but he would rather be dead."
Standing in front of the door he looks straight up to the sky.
The moon appears so big and bright,
and the sky is not dark on this night,
No, it is filled with distant suns and other worlds,
each with a wish resting within,
and the desire for each wish burns as equally as its star.

Part 2: Alone at Home
(Starring Andrew)

Laying in the big arm chair facing the window,
watching the midnight moon shine dimly through the rain,
thinking to himself of the earlier hours,
when he had finally come to know the origin
of his friend Matthew's pain.

"We were sitting on the bed,
talking and listening to music,
just killing away the time.
Then when that song came on,
he moved closer and tried to commit his crime."
Thought Andrew.

Thinking back, he remembered:
His room being filled with that sudden stillness,
the gentle twanging of gentle groove,
the rising smoke of vanilla incense,
Matthew longingly mouthed "Together?"

With reminding eyes "But it's not that innocent!"
"I replied while shutting the window," Andrew recalled aloud.

Those thoughts lingered in his head for a moment or two,
as he had no idea of what to do.
So he remained laying in the chair,
watching the grey rain clouds slowly roll past the dim moon.
"He's walking home now, I hope he knows I care..."
Whispered Andrew, "But I just won't be there for...us!"

Part 3: A Windowed Room
(They merge)

The candle light flickered from across the room. Swift dancing shadows helped take the focus from all of the other thoughts in their minds. Scrunched paper napkins left mangled and dirty from their duty, lay in abandonment. Crevices and folds belonging to everything in the room, seemed to mingle between darkness and light, as the shadow of that light danced on. All of these things, with rising, rolling grey smoke from the incense, gave that moment, that room he called his own, a strange and yet compelling feeling.

Trembling voices, eager yet weary responses darted back and forth past all that lay, flickered and drifted between their faces. His mind raced and raged again, once more arising the desire to stab it with a knife. All things around them seemed to be so near and touchable; especially those dark majestic eyes that stared back. A cool breeze gently sent the curtains fluttering. Every single detail around them suddenly didn't seem to matter enough to be noticed. Every memory of all those walks together admiring that night sky, alit with stars; the brilliant moon and rolling grey clouds-the closeness, the shared view overtook them. Their attention falling to the entrancing, tingling sensations of caressing skin, shadows dancing on his penis, as it was pulled from un-zipped pants. Finally that music they both wanted to live together, was whispering its melody in their ears and finally that touch he wished for upon that shining star, had seen its birth!

Slowly opening his crying eyes,
facing the window as he sat in that big brown chair and
gazed out at the world and that moonlit road before his house.
Here he was once more, alone at home.
Again reminded of it by his apartment's biggest windowed room,
haunted and tormented by the longing that it opened up to him.

"I ask myself so many times, why?
I'm not sure how much longer I'll care.
This amazing flame inside, he always seems to douse,
with my tears and leaves me to that moonlit road to roam alone."
With the escape of a long, hard sigh,
Matthew's head fell back on the chair.
Tears soaked their way down his cheeks,
His long black hair lay draped over his shoulders,
as his gaze never left the moon and star lit, grey cloud drifting night sky.

With a startle, Matthew quickly pushed his hair back into a pony tail
and answered the sudden knock at the door.
It was Andrew, "I'm sorry... let's give it a try. Even if we fail,
we'll be friends, forever more."
And with that, he took Andrew's hand and said:
"Come, I have it perfectly planned."

Glory Lies

I could write it all down,
but it's all yet to be found.
Follow the feeling,
wander the river,
know my reason,
remember forever.

What will it take?
So many thoughts shared with you,
maybe that's the mistake.
Now what can I do,
for you, for me?

So many people,
seem so fake,
maybe it's how I see;
drowning as I drift under a lake.
Never really making any sense,
now I'm lost without a breath.

Got to last another day,
so damn sick of trying to find the way,
positions meaningless in my mind.
So very kind of you...
Trusting me to die in this lie.
Oh you're my confession, my decision and prison.

Melody Calls

Walk along these magnificent corridors;
They're arched so beautifully high and
so wide and bright from the sky's light.
Feel the music all around,
hear the echo from every which way.

Stand and turn a full circle,
from which way does that organ play?
From whom do these haunting melodies pulse?
As if his heart felt true love,
at the instant it died.

You're in the maze now seeker;
found your way this far.
Strength and patience stand as your tests now.
Pick which way you'll follow the music,
and hope you'll meet the composer too!

Turns and twists take your curiosity and turn it to daunting task,
blandness seems to have covered it all.
Just keep on treading, swollen feet and all,
to that composer and hope he has eyes for you.

But would you dare disturb his play?
Shifting his seemingly endless focus,
from sending forth the melody
which fills these corridors.
That, would you do?

Perhaps feeling its enchantment over
you would give reward.
The music is the guide,
the composer is its passion and
the audience is led to feel its magic and love.

To You

Keep the thoughts from swirling in my head
and focus on what lies ahead.
I see your face through the storm,
it seems one more step will do me in
but trees bud after the winter as ever.

Your face keeps me up, gives me the feeling that I can win this.
I only think of how beautiful it will be there with you,
my body stings from frost bite in the cold,
to know you is to know warmth, I want to be there with you, to be in your glow.
Each step I take buries everything in my past deeper,
each step I take lead's me closer to what it was that kept me going,
each step I take leads me closer to you.

The Dancer's Sanctuary

Wander the rooms of your house,
look from side to side feeling so brave.
Shout out and jump in the air without embarrassment,
toss and turn and pose in front of that mirror.

A smile cuts its way across your face,
the sweat trickles down,
you feel like a talent has brewed in you,
and there's a world of things you could achieve with it.

Now swallow hard as your mind settles when you sit,
wipe the tears and your lips.
Don't want the gloomy look to set like concrete,
sigh a breath and hope for death,
while you give yourself another shot on the floor.

The stillness booms like thunder,
the emptiness sends a sharp stinging pain through your head.
Get up and walk around,
loneliness grips your heart, leave's you gasping for breath.

Inward sighs bring back the brutal lies,
which have sent you crashing to the ground.
The price you paid for the pain you hold,
oh how it left you broken.

But none of this crosses your mind at all.
No, you let it all fall from consciousness,
instead you dance and groove.
Posing in front of that mirror without a single fear.
Everyone asks you how you do it,
how you last a single day,
if only they knew, that each movement keeps a certain
thought down and out for the moment.

The Brutality of Truth, Life & Irony

Walk that road every day of my life,
seems to me there is no way out.
I call out your name for help,
but your too far away to hear my cries.

So I trudge along this lonely road,
thinking of all the stories that's been told.
I really don't care to think about the hate and lies,
and I really can't seem to think of a salvation.

A boy rides his bike past me,
to the dirt I push him and steal it away.
This touches nothing in me,
as I think my hurt is worse than his.
As I become the monster of our childhood years.

Out of your mighty castle you come,
bringing with you all my life's secrets,
exposing to the masses my fraudulent heart.
Now, isn't it ironic that I've made all these mistakes,
in trying to be with you... the one who exposes and ruined me?

And I lay in my cold jail cell, staring at the wet, dripping ceiling,
thinking to myself... I never knew it was you at all,
"Oh dear God," I gasp, "I am the clueless man."

A Straightforward Cry

In this life of ours, what do we really strive for?
Can the moment achieve focus?
If our dreams have already been achieved a million times,
we live, eat, sleep and die then, right?
Other than that, all we have is entertainment,
that's it, that's everything our entire lives are composed of.
That's why our reality is so brutalizingly lonely.
We as humans feel grateful for our "superior intelligence",
but really it's all a self-contradicting, self-destructive existence.
A tear finds its way down my face again, again and again.
So maybe this is just my loneliness talking here,
perhaps later when I'm in higher spirits I'll feel like,
this dark part of my life will be surpassed,
and I'll feel like I've covered some good ground.
How meaningless that frame of mind is,
I'll never be capable of measuring,
it's only proof of how life goes on,
how it passes by everything that's happening in our lives,
and brings us all closer to death.
Something that all of us must inevitably face in the end.
So it's just best that I face it now,
to reach out and grasp the icy hand of death,
and let it pull me under and away from this thing we call life.
Because for what purpose do we live?
To continue this miserable existence?
To live and die without a cause?
And, if we do decided to die for a purpose,
and those what we die defending,
in turn die defending and in turn who they fell to defend,
fall themselves,
then isn't it all just a vicious cycle?
One that can never really be stopped or prevented?
There is no point to anything, just principles for perfection.
Perfection is just comfort and entertainment.
And tell me, what point are those two things?
To make us feel good and at ease for the moment.

Yes, at ease until we are taken under,

to lay with the cold lifeless body of death for evermore.
And in that fate, we will not know, nor ever achieve our higher plateau.
Because we died trying to get there,
then we realize that higher plateau is never meant to be reached or achieved,
just thought about and pursued.
So that we continue this miserable existence of ours forever and ever and ever
amen.

Murky Water of the mind

My mind floats around,
all the tangled webs that are my thoughts.
Through the murky water,
it never seems to latch onto any of them.

Oooh, the meaning to everything,
seems too impossible to comprehend.
You travel and swim through the murky water,
searching for a thought that you can hold on to,
that you can understand and call your own.

Again, you slip by another one,
it all passes through.
There was no meaning or strength in it,
so now you drift through the tunnels once more.
Your contempt is lost to the establishment,
of your sick twisted dream.

At last you secure your feet,
and look around to see,
all of what you have pursued,
is all of which you could never be.

You discover yourself as the enemy,
finally the lies before your eyes,
reveal to you the world to be a place of refuge,
that you would never take.

Instead, you found the fault in everyone,
and would never look long enough to understand.
You were always swimming and drifting though the
murky water of your mind.
With brown, black and bold colours mixed and swirling,
you realize yourself as that which you have been fleeing…
Oh, how you're not so elegant anymore.

Woman: The Undeniable Saviour

My riches and colonies,
that kingdom which I called my own,
has transcended me from the poverty,
in which I've suffered and toiled.

My legions where sold away,
I left behind the loneliness,
of those forgotten days.
I'd crumble to the ground,
wishing I was free from my sea of teary-eyed misery.

Once when I was adrift,
I saw you there in your ship,
a maiden with glowing red hair.
Glimmers of light led me to safety,
oh how your eyes sparkle with brilliance.

In your arms I was held,
the tenderness of your touch,
soothed my soul.
And then I knew you were the one,
which I have weeped endlessly for.

Now when I hear and feel your breath,
it chases away all my wishes for death.
In your arms, by your side.
My only wish is to remain in your arms and by your side.

The Mind of the Lonely (Walker)

See a young man tread about the city streets,
he wears a grim smile that always catches your eye.
Trickles of blood ooze through his facial pores,
headstrong with thought, his face is that of stone.

Wincing in pain a hand grasps his brow,
thoughts are flying furious inside his mind.
Pre-occupied all the time with thoughts and worry,
all the time tending to his thoughts and worry.

Nothing seems to faze him,
biggest decisions made with ease.
But all the simplest actions,
transcend his ability and thus he is left,
again with nothing small for joy.

Now a course begins itself within,
running a path through the streets.
"I need to clear my head." he says,
"The fresh air will ease my despair."

And in the wee hours of the morning,
after wandering in the dark,
you can still see that man tread about these city streets.
Looking for the next place to start,
his next cycle of thought and worry.

Moment of Stillness

The stillness of the moment,
in which I lay upon the earth and await death,
is a comfort, such a comfort to me.

In roadside dirt,
dust flies into my eyes by passers-by,
and blood trickles from my veins.
Lifeline gone to waste they say.

But all that reaches me here are memories,
oh sacred memories.
From which I am protected by the warm breath of death.

Years of youth, in which I would look to the future,
have now turned to old age, as I look to the past.
And I see now, in this still dying moment,
that with each passing day,
the secrets I learned in them,
have all robbed me of the mystery of life.
In return, left me with a small portion of its meaning.

So those years of youth,
in which I would await my time of pride, are gone.
And the days of being a young man,
learning lust and love,
are gone.
The hours spent by my brides bed,
awaiting the birth of my first born, are gone...
And the precious moments I have spent with that child,
and that bride, are gone.

There is nothing left for me anymore,
as I lay protected from the feelings and emotions of life by death.

Salvaging Friends

Time has changed you and me,
but our memories still paint that picture.
Just as we were then,
so happy and free without ever a thought,
about anyone or anything else.

I think back to my childhood,
so many tears and years of pain.
But I remember your company,
you were a place of oasis for me.
We have since departed,
but those memories still stand,
against the test of time.

Now after all those years, how am I supposed to feel?
Just brush it all off and move on?
Call you up and talk an hour or two?
You know it'd all cave again,
oh God those lies came so close to being true,
yes they did almost come true.

But a hope hangs from my heart,
as bright as the moonlight in which I tread,
a vision where we could possibly salvage that?
I don't know, you have others now,
you don't know, I have long since been angry.
Put a rest to this now, for sure.
Just see how we accept it, how we could possibly like it...
Once more?

Death Wish

I want to end this life of mine,
everything I've done was a mistake.
Nothing seems to have a worth anymore,
what does anything matter anyway?
Don't we all die in the end anyhow?

After the blood line continues,
down generations from me,
I will be forgotten just like those before me,
but anyway memory isn't life anyhow.

My family loves me, but there's still a void in my gut,
my friends still talk to me, but what does that matter really?
I'm still alone without a single chance of love.
The hope of finding a lover won't come easy,
I'm a man who still doesn't know his way or origins.

And I thought I knew that love once, but it wasn't really there.
In that moment in which I confessed that
those feelings of admiration where mistaken for love...
I lost it all then, there was nothing left to cling to,
there was nothing left to fight for.

So now I'm all alone,
without a single soul to call my own.
Don't tell me who I have,
don't tell me who is forbidden.
Nothing matters anymore.
Just let me lay upon this dirt road,
and await death in the silence of my mind as I whisper:
kill me, with my life,
so spill from me my life.
So drown me in my life.
The only thing I've got is my life,
only thing I have is this life,
there is nothing now... but this knife.

Sunset Eyes

When there are countless thoughts,
flying furious through my mind,
and when it seems the weight,
of all the loneliness and despair,
will weigh my soul down,
into the black colourless abyss of death,
I stand alone to admire those beautiful rolling clouds.

Alit in the golden arrays of the sun,
as it fades behind those western hills.
And I think to myself,
it'll all get better in time.
With time, everything gets better.

All the wretchedness will disappear,
all the loneliness will fade,
and my life will be left in colours,
as rich as those of that western sky...
...that is my hope.

Faster Than the Eye

Give me time for it to sink in;
all those miles I walked!
I'm too tired and filthy to stand alone so
if that's what you got to do,
then I just don't have it.

This land has promise all over it,
or so they whisper beneath their curses.
See the rats scurry about these city streets,
feel the rivers wash down your face,
as you scurry along tail dragging through the mud.

Feel the delusions hit you at once,
they pull you to recluse.
An entire scene where they talk about you,
over your coffin... as you lay within.
"He was a hurt man; no one knew why.
He embraced everything necessary
yet he was a hurt man."

So I'm pulled back here,
these walls with ugly figures hanging all around.
The ringing music battles the washer's buzz.
Ticking clocks won't be heard,
but they strike like lightning.

Now I lay here in the sludge and dirt,
rain patters over my hide.
A gnawing at my gut takes my last ounce of strength.
As I see it finally it is there,
long round vermin eating its way,
through my eye...and I am blind now.
As I watch so many others willingly fall,
and become eaten by the maggots which squirm
through these streets.

Claylike: Being Shaped By Life: Pt. 1
Absorbing the Path

Through the pane; light filled many
Shadowy places.
Revealing odds and ends of vents
And smokey-flame stained bottles.

The silence blanketing all corners
And openings into his room, suddenly,
Was yanked away.
Piano rolled forth from the alarm clock.
Rolling over closer to the end table,
A long oval shaped ball of clay stretched and
Flattened over it-
Wiping out the sound.

Imprinted were the controls.
Am/pm, set, minute, hours...
They quickly faded as he melded the
Arm back to himself.
What was left was positive energy-
About a palmful of strength gained.

Different sparks of frosty blue,
Sweating red and warm light-brown fluttered
Slowly to him.
Each imprinting and effecting uniquely

After pouring out of bed,
The clay twisted and climbed itself.
Its grey mass transforming to blue, red and brown.
He stiffened a little,
Burned in the largest portion,
And dripped slowly as little pieces
of him decayed off here and there.

The days task now having been remembered,
In commanding sensation,
In feared and embraced feeling.

Part 2: Moving With the Effects

His clay form usually attracted attention.
Situations and temperatures of emotions
were of passionate intensity with him.
Each had its effect and impressions of late drained a little more.
Always the desired mould he dreamed of was focal point.

Impressions were reality,
They would always be there.
But to look upon words of expectations, kindness,
judgement and compassion and absorb yet deflect
simultaneously... this he yearned for.

He wanted to remain as clay.
To know he could birth possibilities and dreams.
A stone zombie was not enticing.
Wearing a rubber suit but being clay within
Would sustain his imagination.
Preservative armour to maintain his shape.
To always know he'd recognize the mirrors reflection.

Pulling himself from this thought,
He shifted through his house-
Grey toned surface gleaming in the sunlight
Beaming in through the window.
Merging food and tools into himself for the day.

Focus to fuel desire was placed upon his ears.
Connection to vulnerability and declarations
Of intention was set to vibrate and ring and
Placed in his pocket.
He'd now watch their effect on his temperature
Of emotional colours.

Down the street and to work he kept his distance.
From eyes and foreign things.
He found it hard to find places, things
And ways for use in making his rubber suit,
Where there were things being stuck and pulled to and fro.

Blue and cold thoughts of his lover made
It slow, ridged going.
Red liquid was burning around each single demand
Each motion set him rolling and rumbling in place.
Swishing alcohol left small pungent drops of
Brown portions behind.

Each contact of eyes on him and his state,
Marked him as prey to their advantage;
As a back pack of led.
These judgements served to enlarge his resolve
With want, need and dread and anger… and hatred.

This state of confliction of intense freezing, burning,
Rotting and softness.
They were all caused by things easily banishable.
When two sets of hands throttled the demon,
Its focus and thus strength was divided and as a result…
Weakened.
Didn't they see that?
Couldn't they help rid him of it
even if only to please themselves?

Part 3: Slip Away From Binding Chains

Ahead stood the pillar,
encrusted with a huge shell.
Its shadow was cast clear across
The surrounding grounds,
Invoking bitterness, stammers and fear.

Through its opening he pushed and heard,
"Once again late for this honour!
Where is any desire for preservation?
You must melt down now.
Drain those distracting colours-
They draw others and thus danger."

Echoing from high above him,
Downward and out the front opening to
Entice nearby ears.
His heart pounded harder,
Barely able to stand it along with the longing.
"Show EVERYTHING! Be manipulatable…
To fit this honour."

A burning glow of red intensified.
Not consuming his blue heartache,
Or brown alcoholic decay but building
them stronger.
Oh and but ever very much stronger.

He lifted his head and announced,
"This badge and hammer I pass over.
For to constrict this burning clay soul,
Is to douse the flame of life and set the mould
Of a stone zombie!"

So freely above those grounds he stood.
The despising, jealous eyes behind him,
Long stretching shadow before him.
Within it was unseen obstacles and poisons.

But many paths led here-
Wounded followers have long since clung
To the angry, love-your-sadness firm
(Manufacturing consuming-recluse since times inception).

He picked the path alit by the sun.
It led over the hill, away from the forest
and onwards for his new world.
There was people to love him there
and for him to love
along with pure, self-sustaining strength.

Human Waste Land

Long narrow path stretches on forever around that bend, but a weakness is spotted from crow's tree-tip perch. Mangled branches form a wall all around keeping you within this dark void. Walk along, treading in rhythm with the beat of your heart while your mind is flying furious with your friend fear. Oh yes, that friend is here, in the moonlit path that leads you astray. He keeps you from thinking clearly with his magical touch. Brings dark blue shadowy figures of trees on either side, keeps you from running by using their mangled twisted arms which draw forth streams of blood from you. The rustling of the grass, has that horrible demon come to slay me here in this terrible void? Could he be more frightening than what I've come to see here tonight? Smooth long howl from where he hides, over there! Turn and run, faster and oh ever so faster does that beating heart of yours pulse. Ahead there's a turn, another army of shadowy mangled figures, feet pounds upon the smashed faces beneath; that are the very earth itself! See the blood flow into the grooves between their faces. Moaning and biting at your feet the howling is with you now, inside your head. It becomes your mind and soul, it's beneath your bloody feet, behind and all around you. Screaming and cold from the still, blood-dampened air. Their clothes lay all about in tattered rags, smothering those faces beneath. Searing pain shoots through everything, what a red man you've become, blood flows down your body, down your arm, to your fingertips. Droplets fall into the mouth and eyes of the earth faces. Crunching and rolling live waves. Bones split as skulls burst with more blood, black tar blood oozing everywhere, like tiny trickles of rain water running across the dirt. The waves roll and smash against the tangled trees whose twisted branches pry and grasp at thee.

Turn and run, you fool! Do not listen nor watch these horrors. The waves toss forth mangled gashed demons, every waves brings more. As they all slowly stand before you, twisted faces and broken limbs but they close in on you. So you turn to flee, trying to battle the waves of flesh and bone. Your wounds brings the rolling after you, to you, inside of you. No longer does the strength of life inhabit, anything at all... it seems to be draining from your eyes and mind now. Falling upon the path, you're swallowed by the rolling waves of contorted bone and rotten flesh. The mangled figures feast upon you. Colour returns to their limbs as they flee, now human, for their new lives as the crow casts his gaze from the murder, which takes them all as victims just before the exit gates.

Their skulls sink back into the ground, the welcome mat is fresh once again for more souls to become nothing more meaningful than the shadows that haunt us all through this life.

The Crows & The Dogs

Long narrow road is this life of mine,
sins plague my hope of salvation.
My thoughts and my mind play the part of my enemy,
don't need your pity...
See, there it goes again.

But it all needs time dear moonlit walker,
Where's your midnight dancers?
Hear the barking in the distance,
witness torn flesh in the struggle,
feel the shrill screams echo inside your head.

Yet I'm still here with you,
in those eyes I see the need for company.
As they gaze upon the bloody mess,
ahead on the path within the moon's heavenly light.

Murdered off were the very last ones you knew.
The beating heart of each torn out and carried off
by the murder with haunting calls.
Raining down on you; the droplets of blood
which stained your clothes were left behind.
It was all you were ever left with,
droplets of love from those who are so much higher.

Fall upon your knees, the dogs tear and gouge at your mind,
consistent barking, pissing in every corner of every thought,
and everyone stays so far away.

Left alone to gaze at ugly crows,
with black and bland bodies burning in the sun.
of course the next to come along,
will be torn to shreds as well.

Journey 2: The Way Back

Days of endless daze.
A thousand times you have come to pass,
and a thousand times you will come to be.

Is there any breach in this system?
Everything dies, everything crumbles with time.
So will this cage around my heart come to pass?
Thoughts of peaceful recluse,
could they become reality?

Shake it off, stay strong for the system.
Break and batter those hands of yours,
all for the dreams you hold,
all for that distant horizon,
all for hope.
That is held so tenderly by you.
This is your price and everyone pays.

You're urged to cut away your tongue,
(from your mouth the leeches are eager to feed from the blood).
Don't make silence your mother tongue like they want you to!
Sure there is only hard ice at night,
but daylight will bring forth water to drink.

So don't think about the empty space inside and out,
or the distance between the highs and lows,
or the difference between the in's and outs.
Just stare ahead at what's laying before you.

You're Always Here

I lay awake at night,
I lay away at night.
I'm so far away from here;
They'll find me right beside you.

My mind wanders through too many places.
I've never really time to know exactly how I feel.
Perhaps that is my blessing;
protection from life's emotions
and funny how it's my curse as well.

I wish all those damn problems,
would all just solve themselves and disappear.
I wish the right words and ideas for a joke,
would have come to me while I sat there at that table.
Looking at you... waiting for a smile.

But once again the people threw their stones,
my contempt swelled and raged and was lit.
The trees all around sending flames into the night's blue sky,
and I followed them away to a distant land where life lingers on.

Don't get me wrong,
I welcome company with such open arms.
I welcome those who wear my shoes,
but there is no time or compassion,
for those who say I'm one of the million alike.
To them I say "If I'm just another in that million,
then where's the rest who you say stand like me?"

In my mind there's a heavenly neon glow
spilling in through the window.
Over your body as it moves ever so slightly
with your breath of life as you sleep.

Life's Longing

When the reason to continue fades behind this persuasion,
I'll carve the canyons, ride the rivers that will flow,
and never look to where I'm headed.
As I'm bound for a mindless abyss.

Oh the light is fading now and
I can't see the reason for this as I drift to sleep peacefully.
There is no sign of what dreams are coming,
but I'll count on them before I look to tomorrow,
oh endless tomorrow.

Won't you take me when you go?
I want escape from this longing,
from a life found dancing with the mind
but eluding the body.

Gloryful Creation

Here I lay in wait,
my heart beats down my time.
I don't look to the future,
Lord only knows where it goes,
and all I've done has led me here.
There's nothing in my past to fight for.

All my emotions,
all those notions of which I've spoken
don't soothe me anymore.

So I simply drift along,
with the river that flows from my eyes.
Drifting through the trees,
through the very heart of the jungle,
it beats in rhythm with mine.

There's thunder claps,
and rainstorm wave crashes,
the trees are all battered and felled.
My face is torn as words are sworn,
and the blood is drawn once again.

Hope still lingers in my heart,
that I'll reach the glorious meadows,
where I'll gaze up at sun and sky,
and bathe in the twilight of moon and stars.

Not have I seen you yet,
but there are bright warm times,
and there are dark cold times.
So I know you are there for me always,
For through both this vision remains.

Enemy Mind

Working, slaving every day.
Thinking to myself there's got to be a better way,
a better way than this.

And all I've got to say is...
You could die for all I care,
for all I care.
And you could break down right now,
and cry for all I care,
for all I care.

Oh... Where were you?
Where were you when there were just so many things
raining down on me?

Broken and bleeding I fell to the ground,
I looked and I listened but there's still no sight or sound to you.
So I picked myself up and walked through the forests,
climbed up the trees but still couldn't sense anything of you.

There was no one anywhere,
no one anywhere for me.
Began to think it all a conspiracy,
conspiracy against me.

No one around to give a damn, conspiracy!
Working and slaving all the time,
still not a dime to my name, conspiracy!
All alone in this forsaken city,
people all around but there's not an ounce of pity, conspiracy!
So many faiths, so many churches,
but there's only one God... conspiracy.

I know my mind at ease,
is so very different from my mind at work.
And from my mind at what I love,
and from my mind at what I hate.
and from the mind I should have.

Travelling Within

My time is so fast,
my dream is so slow.
Now why would I feel ashamed of it?
I'll let anyone in to see.
Countless miles await my travel and
As many faces will transit their concept.
But it's a journey set for obstacle tops;
Feel the fish tug and pull the line.

Just shout.
Just look, listen, feel
and work it out.
you know it all can serve you.

So there's a long way to go,
but hey, the long hard road holds all the knowledge.
My eyes can be found upon the bottoms of these feet;
So gesture towards no horizon lest you never reach here.

Just shout.
Just look, listen, feel
and work it out.
you know you can make it.

My All

What if I don't make it?
What if I fail?
It's better than going pale,
from holding my breath and never taking the leap.

They preach focus on tomorrow,
they say it's the only way to avoid the sorrow and despair.
Always trying to be better than what you are,
always trying to be someone else.
I'm not perfect nor your plateau.

Where everything fits so lovely,
and everyone knows how it all goes together.
Where their thoughts never drift away from their
faith or focus.

So now I've said it,
I'll never figure out the puzzle of life.
I'll never love everyone who steps in my sight.

I live for my mind and not yours.
My thoughts are my children I nourish them.
I let them show me their treasures,
and answer their questions truthfully.
I never lie before or to them because
I've come to realize it's the only way
new thoughts will come my way and show me through this life I live.

Passionate Flame

Strangle hold minutes tick away my life.
The substance is so spacey dizzy,
but the trip down I love...
Everything is so out there down there.

Feel good I will,
I'm battling the doubt.
Scorching flame inside flickers,
only want to make it bigger...
It'll never doubt so I fuel it now.

The dark monsters at night,
I cast into the flame.
Laughing faces at me,
I cast into the flame.
Daily highs and lows,
I cast into the flame.
Everything outside the moment,
burns up and away...
Black smoke through the sky.

Nothing in my way now as this
fires built so high.
standing free in its glow.
My world's reduced to ashes,
I'm truly alone now as I cry.

Modern Day Mindset

Hey now yeah.
He's been disappearing within sight again,
while insight lingers everywhere.
Just sitting, waiting
for it to hit him.

Same old way it's always been,
Aluminium sobbing and discarded in the mud,
As Iron's worn against his breast
(beneath his garments).

Restraint has been demolished,
moderation is our forsaken God.
We want everything all our lives and
have all undefined "overindulgence".
Obsession is overtaking us.

Without Resolve

Into a moment it all may crumble,
Flashing hot as defeat looms.
Perhaps everything high should tumble?!
Bury all mirrors, destroy perfection,
And at the end sit alone.
Middle of the room.

Subdue the monophobic, claustrophic serpent.
Drag in air,
Feel your chest expand.
Throbbing back is all the tumultuous thoughts.
Throbbing in is all the bites of venomous fangs
In your mouth.

Feeling you cannot handle the racing-
Of course all this urgency was evident!?
Settled by the deep pond,
Under a huge weeping willow is this reality.
Clutch hard your treasured, sympathetic
Disadvantage.
Shift about in that chair.

Hand in hand, feel the frenzied venom coursing.
Urgency is squeezing your lungs from air.
Oh how one who cannot sit alone in a room
and feel peace is one who lives in utter hell.

The Beloved Computer System

Justice only ever rears its head,
when someone has wound up dead.
No care for the soft, sensitivity in any of us.

Just kill all the wonder and mystery,
leave us all numb to our destiny
and destined to accept a pitiful fate.
One that no person can endure...
But wait! We can!
Being the inhuman robots that we are.
With flashing red, orange & green lights and sirens sounding.

When your program has been infected,
We're held at distance and refused resetting;
Being now a threat to their system.
Caterpillar the climber;
With your boot prints left on my face.

Free to Roam

Feel the rain, feel the rain,
soaking through your brain.

Feel the rain, feel the rain,
as you walk through these wet city streets,
hoping there's people you could meet.

This moment will end soon bringing
in the morning all of those same old things to do.
So stand in the twilight of the streetlight
smiling at the faces so eagerly.
So stand in that twilight, contemplating another disgrace.
Time keeps on passing by,
contempt races through your heart.
"Who needs them anyway?" you say.
Forever alone, free to roam,
forever alone, free to roam.

Free to roam...in the rain,
and to stand in the twilight waiting for life.

Confusion Turned Contortion

Burning flame scorches the air,
nightly sky an orange glow.
Staircase wider and more inviting than that bed.

Lonely passage ways,
barren of souls
even though there's millions about.

Deep within the battle rages,
rages with fury,
rages without remorse.
The bloodshed and strength
I hate... so it doesn't build my fire.

Just one lonely step after another.
Description wearing thin as it builds within.
Feels like I might explode.
Feels like I might die.
Where do I run? Where do I hide?
How do I fight? How do I cry?

My Inner Creativity

Don't waste, don't waste.
Don't waste, don't waste.
Don't waste, don't waste,
don't.

Dimensional freedom,
directional choice of
the invisibly fast animals.
When before them,
You are sent to the ground,
On the ground, into the ground.

My sewing machine,
allows it all to arise,
left hand brings it all forth,
battles with my right.

Piercing and waving together,
my perfect blanket is complete.
Beautiful designs, delicately soft.
Keeps me from freezing,
from the rush of wind,
from those invisibly fast animals.

Wires torn,
body scorched and seared.
Now I piece together,
with my sewing machine.
Now I have my image,
Through those animals who have disappeared.

Youth in Age

Down these streets,
there's meaningful laughter in the faces.
Jack rabbit speed it soars and is
impossible to catch.

The invitation seems irresistible.
Glitters like gold,
but I'd be left the fool.
So I think I'll just remain in the harmless admiration.

And when my eyes are searing, burnt and blind.
When the un-navigable darkness
becomes my place of refuge,
safety will once again hold all our hands.

Will it lead us to truth? Yes.
There won't be any temptation remaining
and discovery will find me.
I'll kiss those fast faces,
my heart will race at time lost and to the infection
of laughter which will once again create my youth…
For my second chance?

Where Our Thoughts Lay

Down that path
through pure darkness into the unknown
where the minds of children linger.
Presence may be sensed;
But only by he who knows his mind.

Even though the twilight night may seem
to some a blessing;
a curse is closer to what it really is.

For when the night pulls you
out of your warm dwelling
and into its cold, invisible surrounding,
all the parts of your mind,
walk down that path with imagination once again.

Off to each side there are little clearings,
where all the games of old are played again,
they never really cease.

Here in the night of eternal youth we are held forever.
Never to experience life beyond memory.
In all its love and pain.

From Within We Conquer

Uncertainty grounding,
here it rises forth once more.
Little period now... now you know it?

From the wreckage within my sorrow must be torn.
Never seeps out all its own, forever so captive; confined.

What recluse can be seen? Do I belong to it or it to me?
Can't seem to sort it out, here I go again, again.

Now I'm held up,
marvellous pillars with faces of stone.
No hearts, no minds within...
Just carved stone.

One place to overlook it all,
only one place from which to fall.
Fear builds itself within me,
all through everything I knew.

It's all from here now, let go.
Feeling special rids need of that place,
walk on from that mess.

Chaotic Orange Glow

All I remember now as I think back,
was the spaced out daze surrounding us.
The long highway stretching on so far,
and (of course) the stereo sent forth waves of hypnotic melodies.

Yeah, feeling fulfilled as that song played.
The battle within subsided (miraculously) for once.
Humming along while we whizzed by.

Countless things we could witness,
nor was there any place forbidden.
But of course, the big orange ball,
bounced and collided with the treasures
we saw that night.

The police pulled us over, glowing up and radiating it did.
Recluse, the survival instinct, kicked in for me (as always).
Desperation and plotting of escape,
and hope for freedom, for him.

So I stood, so still and rabid.
There were three white chariots,
manned by deadly gladiators all around.
Clouds of breath in the air from the horses noses.

Time seemed to stand,
mighty balanced without the slight sways.
That never made it any easier. Couldn't see clearly,
so I talked to no one.

After describing my situation,
realization finally kicked in.
I looked around... here I was.
Somehow in the midst,
of that warm orange glow.
Panic? Perhaps, but not then.
No, instead there came a sudden moment,
I found sense in that chaos (suddenly) and it all fit.

Order of Our Worlds

I've been alone everywhere I've gone,
Through the woods and down all those trails.
So long have I searched for that place
to find that answer but to no avail.

More so now than before I take moments to look around
at the people, their faces and how they are.
Evidence of their search for that answer, too, can be seen.

We are all human.
With curious and wandering minds.
Perhaps it may stray,
but the sight keeps it all going.

I know by taking care of things,
my world will come together,
maybe not any clearer.
But at least just a tad more tolerable.

A Merge of Special Places

No more on the mysteries.
Forever shall the corridors of my mind remain vacant.
Large, marble windows,
beautifully arched and overlooking meadows.
Luscious green cascading boughs,
rivers trickling from mountains,
rabbits scampering upon the grassy knoll.

Rolling clouds in a baby blue sky,
all alit in that golden sunset.
From picture windows these things
I look upon no more… no more.

Walk down that corridor,
down to the den.
Gentle dim flickering light,
laughter and bare feet with you.

No more,
must I look upon happiness,
with longing eyes.
for I am there; here with you.

Sorry

Sorry if I never, for them, seem to care in the end.
Sorry if I don't have a million friends.
Sorry if my feelings fail to run as far as the streets.
And there's a million people I've never thought to meet.
All I ever think of is you.
There's no one else I want to see or do.
Sorry if I'm not the world.

Sorry if I may be any of those faces that bring back memories for you.
Guess I'm just the clueless, devastating Ken doll.
A real sweetheart for one and all.
With a heartbeat of a mind (always beating out the thoughts).
Perplexing, transcending, insipidly complex.

Sorry for the fumbling mistake I make next.
Let's hope it's going to be awhile to it...from here.

Deja Vu Fate

Sometimes the daze takes me strong,
laying upon my bed helplessly.
I wander the corridors of my mind,
seeing all those places again.

Oh God,
their sight leaves me with my confusion.
Strength no longer an ally to me.
No, instead he turned tail and fled,
and left me here for dead.

Pain shooting throughout my comprehension,
everything seems so far away
and as those faces flow past my souls prison.
I gaze out my neon and glitter lit window view.
I see, once again, them going while there's nothing I can do.

Our Place

Sometimes I walk these streets late at night.
Such a battered, troubled, scarred man, yet I fight.
Their laughing faces haunt me always,
seems I'm chained to them forever.

Through those doors, it's full once more.
My eyes with tears, here again?
My God, how am I taking more?
As they slam behind me (just like before).

You're with me at work, filling me with life.
Turning to see your face, realizing you're out there again.

Who really knew we'd be here?
All the willows and daffodils weep and wilt.
Nothing within is growing anymore,
just a lot of tilled soil, scars and empty sunrises now.

As we climb up into bed,
with the morning sun across your chest.
All the grooves and shadows invite to search.
I spot all the dark and damaged places which
have remained with you since you were a little boy.
We fall asleep to the songbirds and blind to the morning light.

Where You've Gone

You were always there with me.
Conversations soared between us through the silence
when things would settle to a quite state once again.
You'd come by to see how I've been.

I've never really thought to prove you wrong.
Just so busy fighting for it all.
Now that I've set down my sword,
with the blood stains and scars in their places
I listen and hope you'll come again.
Feverish prayer begs to have no scars found upon you;
Please say you've maintained that distance from this battlefield.

Don't leave me here.
On this lookout tower,
with the world so far out of reach.
Just like you seem to me.

From a Lookout

It's funny sometimes how we know certain things,
and yet they elude us.
So busy trying to keep in the race,
that we leave it all out of sight,
out of mind again, right?

I'm trying to find that love once more
but my past is not that place, they say just keep going.
Well I see the houses drifting further and further
in the back of my mind.
And I ask myself, while I gaze to there trying to see
the warm glow of my old room window,
through the massive oaks and poplars.
With the drifting warm, summer midnight wind.

How am I getting any closer,
when everything I've ever known seems
to be drifting further away?

Who are you, or anyone, to say on what or where my fate lays?
When it seems that the backwards view through which I look,
reveals to my naked eye's, exactly what I need to see...
That urgency for hope.

Importance of the Journey

A mouth speaks endless words.
Forever wandering the halls leading to joy.
Never quite settling; just bouncing and blowing
wind for always, right?

They say life is self-discovery.
What you see in others,
they may not see in themselves.
Perhaps they're not ready to understand.
Hush no don't tell them, not yet anyway!

Yes as flame is for a candle, so is this.
The journey to get there is so very long and hard.
But, although you wish to cut it short, don't!
We all know while you walk the lands of earth and soul
the mountains and minds all open their heights and sights
for you to see; they unlock the mysteries.

If you cut the journey short,
these important sights and scars will lose much guiding effect.
Yes perhaps these lessons could be given as knowledge,
But what enters through the eyes is held closer to
ones heart than that through their ears-
Only approachable through and
thus touched by the hands of experience.

Nourishment with Reflections

Familiar places, instinct kicks in.
Knowledge is a detail, fact and the cold hard reality.

Here I am continuously treading my nightly paths,
eyes gazing upon the sky.
They're so heavy now with work on the mind especially.

Huh, well don't worry kid perhaps that day will come,
better be soon because that reality
has had a long, lonely time to settle and harden in.

So I breathe deep and heavy,
life never guiding me with familiarity and it
feels I'm always changing everything...
...everything except that tattered frayed pictured poster dream.

Some would say I'm ambitious,
others say I'm a man of persistence.
But I just know these eyes have not graced this
old world enough yet to settle in on a dream fitted to forever.

Well it's a hoard of stones now,
tossing and skipping them across the lake.
Each sinking to the bottom and are covered with mud
as I'm desperately trying to wash away the filth.
I examine the pebbles and perhaps piece it back together.

Reaching in, getting wet,
reflections show me understanding is not an enemy.
Seeing I may never unbury some of the oldest treasures,
these new pebbles, and those still in my hand,
may be used for aiming to future dreams.

A Saviour

Here I lay alone,
deep inside the caverns of my mind.
All the trickling springs merge together,
along the shore side he kneels and takes a drink.

As always the wind of my minds heavens,
seems to drift every which way except forward.
Leafs skater about my feet,
insects migrated to them,
up body and inside my mind,
those worms where eating away at my brain.

I thought insanity was forming,
but was it just a fear?
Oh God perhaps I'm just another typical skeptic.
To be different, dear child am I different?

Tired and battered,
I retreat to my point of pondering.
To my knees I fell,
it was all shattered, broken and devastated.

Sitting on your couch tears filled my eyes.
Confusions squeezed at my heart
and direction was certainly gone with the current.
Now sitting in that pond, gazing at me behind laughing eyes;
suddenly I felt so alone as I cried.

Dear child, isn't it all grand and funny now?
How I was on the brink of pure defeat,
on the brink of losing my last ounce of everything left,
and suddenly it was all so dark for me.

Laying upon my face,
breathing the dirt millions had tread upon (here in my mind),
a glimmer caught my attention from across the water.
My body was dry and aching,
My eyes were drained and all but dead.

But still they caught a sight of a certain glimmer.
The splash startled me from drifting into defeat and
curiosity kept my attention and mind alive just enough
to see who it was that was coming to save me.

Dear boy, it was you!
My love, the one and true,
pulled me up and brought me into the living water,
and helped me drink just as you had taken a drink yourself.

Now we bathe together,
live, laugh and love forever.
Your soul, I want it,
that's my new direction,
it's my goal.

Now when I sit away from you,
my mind drifts to the dirt again.
Telling me everything's bad and not well,
but I know different.

I tasted the water that was ours,
I felt refreshed.
I look into your eyes,
I see that's what you felt too
from me? Can that be?

Every day my love renews.
Stronger and stronger I'm settling into myself.
Your eyes, your sky filled with colours and light.
Heading off into my sunset,
together so perfectly away into that sky.

The Truth Behind A Man

Hear the willows whisper your name,
Leave all your swirling thoughts behind,
As you climb up those branches
Leaving the world below.

Sway from side to side.
Hear the creak as you fear your seat will crack.
But it holds strong so you let it slide.
As you stare up into the sky once more…
For the millionth time.

So many white cotton shapes,
They all could be anything you'd like.
Now let's pretend they're the first sight to a beautiful evening.
Let them pull from your mind all the things
that you find so very impossibly hard to find.

A stillness of contentment with a friend
you'd like to think could be reached once again.
A memory where that lonely little ball doesn't go crazy
and knock it all down inside your world
leaving mess scattered about once more.

Deep invading breath sent forth as a sigh of life.
Knowing that sadness and corner void of light,
Which no man can ever fight because it's in everyone
Is making this moment of blissful escape such a lonely prison.

Cry a silent curse from knowing your peaceful moments,
only come when the hardships drive you into them.
So really, you don't have a peaceful heart.
Just a sad guilty conscious for not pushing all of this,
The hatred, depression, constant loneliness away in a constructive manner.

Dreams

Day after day that same cycle keeps going.
No matter what I look forward to,
It doesn't seem to ever really change.
My dream is found somewhere down
a two way street;
comes by way of thievery from the glass
encased podium one way or
found and dug out from the boot imprinted mud the other.

Competition never solved anything.
I guess we're all too desperate to stop and think.
Whenever I do decide to remain calm,
standing alone is the result.

Going back and reading all of my poems.
I can see how deeply I believe in fair chances.
They say there's no such thing as original anymore,
Which is fine because I'd rather be relatable.

The open road beckons me; the car a luxury to use.
Especially when I'm fleeing my own human half
because time has always been an ugly bastard.

Always slowing down just enough,
to make me feel helpless to reality.
I don't believe in fate or destiny.
I believe in the possibility to win against all odds.
Call it strength or karma,
I call it dreams,
and I will awake to them one day as my truth.

Fugitive on the Run

Every place I go,
everything I know;
always seems the same
and there's never anyone to blame.

Driving in my car,
no matter how far I travel
I wonder how long the road ahead stretches
before leading me to escape from all my sins.

It keeps on coming around again.
Things seem to be rotting,
the past is back again.
But my end is always staring me in the face,
a lot more lately.
And no matter where I'm headed,
seems like there's no way to forget the sins,
or the punishment due to me,
in which I dread.

Travelling Son

When you're on your own,
And are having too much fun
To realize you're alone.
If you have not the faintest idea
Of where people are and still
Yet have not a care then go.

Then travel my son.
There he goes; my travelling son.
Can you see the gold and perhaps read
his story being told?
There in the sky his words are worth priceless
treasure I'm sure.

Free above the white peaked mountains,
Over it all.
It will always win,
It will always call.
The Golden sun, urging me to
be this travelling one.

So, God, resting in the winner's circle,
surely mercy must have your heart captured
When you look upon this tragic searching boy,
who among so many; is alone.

So, God, will you remember
when you turn your attention to the next?

Lucifer's Fall

Here in the silent stillness
A thunderous reality booms.
It dwells within darkness
filling the corners with void.
Never truly showing itself just showing
Faint awareness of eternal lasting death.

When you ask truth to be spoken,
His lips remain still.
There were outreached hands,
But he shut his eyes to them.
Gifts of love were offered for his heart,
But he just refused them and walked
back to the long gone start.
Our concern for him fell away from
Heart and mind.
Now we must find him and steal his breath,
For he desires nothing but death.

Internal Confliction

I've found in life that some people very quickly decide whether they like you or dislike you. There is no meter, scale or any measure of rating really... either you yield complete respect and allegiance instantly (yet even this isn't enough most times) or they exile you from ever gaining any amount of recognition or acceptance.

Upon watching you and shooting out their tests, if you've kept their interest this long, and they decide the performance is well enough... you're in. Things are shared explanations given and support and leniency is found amongst you. They show understanding and accept it from you in return. Respect and value is really there.

But being dismissed without a chance or to fall to their tests is to know that over time no amount of hardwork, efficiency or kindness you pour out for them will ever be enough. The things you've done well are achieved to silence or to comments of how they would have done so differently. When you accomplish access to that part of yourself which is THE BEST, your best, and give it constantly they say you're working against them (making them look bad so to speak). But beyond this you continue, pushing through their outright disapproval and go to grasp your goal alone. Surprise shifts from relief when suddenly they promise help for the goal to disappointment when this carrot forever dangles just out of reach. So in a final stand you try connecting with them, you share observations, vulnerabilities even. Yet all is met with dismissal. You are left invisible to them and alone.

The back of the line is where you fall, seeing your due respect mocked, discarded and very nearly all but forgotten. The ones whom are "in" (who are liked) revel in their exclusive club of humanity before you; unaware or intentionally ignorant to what it was which brought this to them. They are tools manipulated, used only to insult and deny you farther. These graced ones are built up in such ways to overshadow you. To keep the light away so growth and blossoming won't come.

Over time this whole conspiracy enables you an ability to detach from the care of others opinions. When stances of stone point, passing comments shot viciously and strings, sticks and carrots are found scattered about... search for their own shadowed parts. Always turned towards the darkness, away from the revealing light. The very few fleeting chances to spot them from the corner of your eye are subtle, and theirs are sharp so it is rare to see... but you can spot it.

When you do spot it (the toll their battle leaves), it is very recognizable and many times familiar. Shame is always in war against pride, each claiming need while neither wanting want. Their pride refuses to recognize the helpless, powerless state you've been forced into; there's absolutely no desire to be reminded of when they were there or to admit it. Their shame is wrapped in empathy, seeing you slowly wilt in darkness reminds them of their own screams for resolve. Sometimes this may instil guilt in them. So they are caught up with this internal conflict: build up pride and thicken the darkness or resolve the shame and for once really recognize and accept. It is a hard choice to face! How do you build up that which you also wish to trample?

Enchanted

Her hair flows like curtains
And velvet ropes from the heavens.
Eyes are glowing lamps lighting the
long hallway.
Oh, they show you down to the end and
Safeguard your step over these stairs.

Out in the streets of different stands,
Golden rain through each lamp.
A movie from a warm slow store,
Leaves off the branches out into the wind.

I've come to see her in different
ways, nothings constantly the same.
And I can't get away,
She's got this old time feeling.

Prepare My Place in You

Sitting alone here,
I won't pretend I'm the best you've had.
Only chance I have is to learn and free this heart.
So what if our love dies?
The memories will remain forever,
With us or behind my eyes at least.

Carry on through the pain and
wanting to remove all the marks.
We've (thankfully) forgotten the game,
Now the journey begins.

Tears and crying,
Fears leave us lying.
Why is transformation incompatible with a merging union?

My Time in F.A.L.L.
(Freedom and Lonely Love)

The more I try to be an individual
and do things on my own,
The more you scream at me.

The more I try to be happy with joy
or sad because of making a mistake;
Irritated because I've accidently forgotten or broken
Something (even easily replaceable)
is the more you distance from me
and make me feel useless.

The more I just try to be a human,
Is the more you want me as superman.
Well I'm sorry, I can't be anything more than human
And if that's not enough for you then go fly away.
Defying those odds again.
So much faster and farther from everyone,
Up and away into that lonely freedom that is the empty sky.

I'll just stay here grounded,
Weeping as I know with all my soul
that for once I've actually tried.
And even though it was all in vain,
I won't let on to anyone about my pain.
Because the only place that feels right to turn
Is your shoulder.
Why is it so cold to me now?

No More Words

What has been done to bring me here?
No one knows the unspoken words.
Only God, he knows your thoughts evil fiend!

I am not the enemy here,
Do not expect to back me into a corner of fear.
Patience is wearing thin,
The journey to nowhere is nearing its end.
Keep on fighting as the still-tongued warrior!

Slashing into the hearts of men,
Spewing blood over travelled paths.
Words rendered low and useless now.
So there will be no cries for help?

My left shoulder has been cracked.
My left ankle's torn and swollen from breaking.
Knowledge of the battles purpose is lacking.
Faith of victory I hold close to my breast,
Or else it'll all sound and end the same.
Fight without all of their blind causes.

A Mother's Words

Here in the light of the moon,
Where countless things spill into the senseless beyond.
Many things are resented and lost;
Others are battered and kept alive.
Some of them for the joy of rage;
Others for the hatred of the pain.
But they both suffer.

Every day is always the same,
Nothing ever bringing them to fame.
One more breath will bring them to the dead line.
Because we rocking on the edge of tomorrow,
Simply because we cannot find the will for today.
Clocks about to tick it flat out,
Now we're all in line for the final doubt.

He's going to speak the verdict,
Wait right there I know you can.
We'll speak it before you say it.
Speak it before you say it.
Give me an honest chance,
A second chance.
A fighting chance to fit my reason in somewhere.

But don't think of me or all I say.
I'm just happy to find my way with you yeah.
You know it; I'll do anything you want me to.
I don't mind, I don't care.
I don't dare to say no to you.
Because I am so afraid of having everything
I do for you in vain.

Loveflower

Too much time always leaves me an empty minded boy they say.
If only I would pick up the stone helmet and
pound away at something constructive.
That wall of protection around my heart and life would take shape, right?
Well, I'm sorry if I can never seem to find the perfect words to say.
Even more so, I'm sorry that I just can't seem to show enough
strength to act on them.

Our relationship has had its pit falls and shares of bad luck.
Now that I look back at your life,
I realize one thing that scares me so much inside.
People who drifted in and out of your life's path,
Only did so when you were taking your rest alongside of it.

Off to the side you've been with me,
Seeing so much that you didn't before.
On the verge of making it all up to be so grand and better than before.
On the edge of a cliff that could claim you and would pull you into its cycle.

I'm sorry if it seems I'm the door this cycle has been using.
Things never really seem to get done,
Life marches on with time.
Theirs is a relationship built to last.
I'm hoping beyond every fibre of my being.
Beyond anything I've ever known or experienced,
Out of reach of my elders and out of the reach of my pain and past.
Away from the smothering foggy haze that has always taken me by storm,
That we could last like that too!

I don't know everywhere you've ever been.
Perhaps bits and pieces will find their way to me.
Our love is not obsession, our love is not gratitude,

Nor is it dependence.
Our love is not defiance nor do I see it's a potential victory.

I see our love as an obsession to show all those people who have
Ever stood in our way that we are beyond grateful that the dependence
We have on each other to defy all those, to defy everything that has
Ever held us down is a potential victory.
Our potential victory, because alone love cannot bloom.

Bash Your Burning Brain

Always searching for the right time and place,
Hoping we can change up the words a bit.
Never wanting to sound or appear the same,
Every soul in the world wants to be that much better.
They want to stand out that much more,
So they'll be remembered that much longer.

Our mind is a powerful tool,
Always working against us.
It uses time against us,
Devising new ways to bloat our existence
With more needless things.

Willow trees blow in the wind,
Leaves falling upon the rolling, tossing waves
which surround it.
A ship fights its way to shore.
The madness will ensue once it has docked.
Pray to be possessed to fight the odds.
Drifting current full of fish;
Oh unfeeling fish.

Wooden, bark covered snakes swim about,
In through the holes of every space.
Holding fast to every race.
Defeating all competition,
Winning every prize.
Emerging from pure defeat,
Descendants of angles.

Painting pictures with these words,
Excalibur was flung to the ground bent and useless.
The pen gloated and wrote out its glory note of victory.

Here I sit, having finally lost all of my contempt,
Only to be trapped to an even more powerful enemy.
The pen, the words, the thoughts… my mind!
So maybe if I end it the next time,
Just before the pen wins by slicing my heart in two,
With that mighty sword, this vicious cycle will end.

Burden the Angel

Some things seem so cement,
But yet they're pure liquid...
I cry for our love.
Because of the mental anguish I am to you,
Because pleasing you has nothing to do with me.
Crying always ends the same.
Feeling alone and misunderstood.
I'm always left to battle the shame,
Always left face down in the mud.

There's never a prayer for the hopeless romantic.
Always something better needs doing.
What am I to you?
Well, that's what my judgement is.

There in school,
I feel it's my fault.
There on the weekends,
I feel it's my fault.
The regret sit with me on the couch,
I'm told it's heavy on you.
I'm told you'll feel bad for me later.
Well just know one thing:
I don't want advice, just a lover.

How am I supposed to feel?
This disease is killing us.
You're only so strong,
Now the time has come to stand back and watch you.
Well my eyes are damaged,
Damaged from crying and observing.
When my saviour would come,
Well here you are now, so why can't I love you?

Why can't you open up to me?

Take a breath, take a walk alone.
See those large iron gates in the distance,
Journey past them to the oak on the hill ahead.
There's a cement gravestone cross,
Cracked and shifted,
A pool of water has formed on the grave.
I fall to my knees,
Hands on the crucifix,
Head bowed and eye's swollen in sorrow.

Again they fall but fail to awaken you.
All the wretched insects that have devoured the body left.
My knees are soaked from the loneliness washing down.

Here on the hill at the cross,
Wishing to God I could have been better for you.
Cursing myself because this disease has buried you.
Desiring more than anything to know if I pleased you at all
or ended the anguish long enough for you to know,
What it must have felt like to be with me without it.

In the beautiful night sky I see a shooting star,
I feel something around me, telling me reflections won't get me far.
Telling me to pick it up and carry on.
With my head still gazing at the dirt I ask "What must I do?"

A brown tanned skin hand reaches to my face,
Pulls my chin up allowing me to see
you're so soothing to look at,
you're so soothing to touch.
I'm sorry that I'm garbage,
Soaking your grave and bothering your eternal rest.

"Don't cry!" you say, "I have always loved you.
Just love yourself."
Gazing at such an angel,
I feel all sorrow melt away.

Innocent Danger Race

Your lips utter lies,
They make me cry.
No freedom for the poet,
You said you'd call but didn't.
How was it supposed to appear?
I just wanted to hear you say it.
To hear from your mouth;
A secret that could possibly explain
what it is under this sun or moon that's holding you from
giving me anything you own that isn't material.

Glass vase on my lap,
Ground and sea fills the air with fragrance.
Tears of lonely sorrow and waiting-in-vain rain
down on it as I call your name.

Up rises the flower,
What kind of power must it have?
Everything was handed to you by me.
So my love, don't burn mine when I reach for yours.

Here upon the dirt and dust,
Empty feelings filling my heart.
But they are kept to create,
Model and sculpt a new start for us.

So now that we're here at this time,
And seemingly ready to go,
I just want to know who will be the first to cross it?
Who'll be the first to start for some loving?

Veinstone

The trail of my mind,
Desires burn his line.
Where are the willows
with the valley doves!?
Nothing could have ever been strong enough to provide.

So I just turn my head,
And stare at the only crutch I've ever known.
Now that your sky is painted colourless
everyone desires with exotic pleasure
to hear your master plan.

Dig and brake the demon within.
You were he who would never give in.
Isn't it funny that it's the same and different!?
Now isn't the purpose digging at your brain?
Swimming across the canals, valleys and luscious green river forests
Just to understand what was the pain that turned you to vainstone.

Now I turned to rock,
Hollow boxes given to me.
Left playing a game that you don't like.
Please don't go out street light,
If so, I'll lose possession of the strength that
is bringing my hope to its maximum height,
That I'll find my way back to my love.

Beaten Space

There was a place in me,
So bright it shone with brilliance.
Millions of times we would sit,
And recount the days of pain and pleasure,
Is it there any longer?

You're so fast?
Doesn't that uncertainty scare you?
You're so brave,
Don't their swords pierce at all?

Never venturing out the door,
But still down to my depths you'll journey,
Just to know what I mean.
Hands tensing as I grip this pen far too tightly.
What energy do you have for me?
It is as great as what you've stored away,
For precious answers that you love more still.

Accessories are wants and we all long to be needs.
And while countless alike monitor the space amidst these;
I just want to be a person.

Curse and think,
Speak and meditate,
What is the difference?
Could a beaten space for me be within you?
I hope I'm still there for always.

Brave Fact

Don't tempt me,
Pages fly.
Think some more,
Thoughts are said to be as evil as the deed.
I bleed in need,
Gritted teeth,
Blood shot eyes.
No humouring or patronizing to me,
Kill me instead.
Kill me dead if that's the case.

No pity,
I go for gold.
I'll make you break my mould.
I leave no choice,
Create and kill if need be,
But never create and meddle with me.

I may be creation,
But you've boiled red my minds conception,
So you won't dispose me?
Okay I'll remember that and blow apart your heart.

Sex, drugs, alcohol, rock-n-roll,
Everything you need to be quick tempered.
Sex, drugs, alcohol, rock-n-roll,
Everything you need to lose a soul.
I hope it's mine.

Not Quite So Sure

I'm not quite so sure what the point is. My mind always seems to wander. Never quite getting over this fascination of theories I have of things that are ancient. Uncertainty is a killer, people killing to find what the next thriller is. Lies and motives hold together our quest for the conspiracy regarding the beginning. It is God and if so, then how so? Was there a time when good and evil worked together? How long has that battle raged? This soul of mine seems to desire answers to what I'm not sure about. Perhaps the flash retro night of long gone, unlived days to me has become my God; I hope it's a sweet one. Little honey for combs or hives that have been commercially bottled and are for sale? Yeah, maybe I'm for sale too? Easily influenced just like my father. People and their desires, the more we fill the more we spill our secrets. I wish they were sweet and free like the natural honey but instead they're manipulated and expensive like the store brand.

Choices of armour? Armour from where? God the physical body. We are from God. I want to see God's body.

A Ghost's Doom

Beautiful night skies, drifting clouds and broken moulds. You know countless chains may be torn as I long from deep within for them to melt off me and seep into the ground. Dear hypocrite entangled in the thought bushes, down there in the valley dip. Could you have been true at one point? Now I feel the rage swell within, smiles crack and tear across this stone glass sorry face of mine. Fearful anger boils and these chains, after all, do melt and seep into the ground. Roots mutinous roots sucked up the boiling red hot liquid, now blood curdling screams echo through the valley as salt pidgins perch upon his head, sending sprinkles upon all his tears and cuts… the exposed flesh bubbles. Busted eyes and the sky is the last thing he sees as the beaks of the pidgins and the shadow of the moon leaves him in eternal pain and darkness. Oh beautiful night sky, rolling grey clouds and a ghostly white figure floating up to the graveyard that is the moon which calls her.

Mesh

A slipping pass is without similarities to death, tear drops crying or fighting it excuses one from socializing and from speech, right? Who was it that was pond off on me and in turn destroyed the trust which was given to me? No fault colours their shade as bright darkness. Earth of lush emerald forests harden like you, scream it now, harden like you, scream it now. This is not good... what has fallen and died? Must I hold this breath of mine in order to find another thrill in the same old things? How many stages? Doesn't your tongue know it's ass from its ears? Surely our mono tone is a hope that I'll bring your now arriving courage, a marvellous halt to the tears that everyone pulls and yanks from me. Purpose, defence, reason and just cause.... are they all important? Don't look at me as if it's died. Life is stages, Life is clay. I'm the Hammersmith. Now isn't that a nailed, pounded-by-the-hammer truth?

Arrogance in Flight

Only on a cool, crispy blue day with wind could men like these be so
successful. Never has such lies been a mould, jewels pulse your heart, why is it
you sit with her and bash? Why more still, is it that you say this is all innocence?
Remember that easy atmosphere? Where the reader and writer were the utmost
allies and confidants? Then why now have the instruments callen? Was not a place
with me in musical silence enough? He took a long, twisted drink of his rum-n-
coke. It would make him look older but it felt natural so he twisted it further. Clues
may be from nothing so are we done killing the clock? Are you counting father
time that way? For Heaven's sake, that boy's way down there along the horizon
shouting "We are it!" So why am I a battered man by you? Set the truth free and
look our way now!

Self-Preservation

Another moment where the point isn't buried,
Deep within my mind.
I was surprised and excited at first but then
That sight set reality in.

Connection to these dreams and inspirations found.
This journeys remainder leaves me reeling.
There's a history and even more sobering… a grand defence!

Glimmering in the blue moonlit rain,
Upon that bridge standing in a handshake: humour with death.
An agreement conspiring against patronage.
So cast aside nothing in relation with me.
I'm not strong nor right but merely searching
for the strength to finally fatally defeat what's ahead.

Insignificance seems ugly and twisted to you,
But what of defence? It's evident before my eyes.
Mine is equal to yours so what is over me?

Give the old!
Tremble-handedly pass it over as you seem turned cold.
Pieces is what I have left to use,
To put it all back together whichever way I like.

There's rarely witness to what's found in sensitive moments.
So no one sees what my pieced work is yet.
Until it's built, I'll soldier on.
Hoping it's a long, long handshake.
Because the emotion of my eyes is worth saving.

Slow Down

Turn your back to the mirror.
In fragility and yearning for love
You put distance between you and me.

Beat it out with that music,
The tongue lashing in each song.
If another's, then kiss!
If mine, then bite!

Passing glimpse of a vision I see.
But it hurts to speak of it so I turn away.
I've been thinking everything in life is an event.
Well it's still better to slow down.
No need found for excessive haste
(especially when standing in place).
Time alone is good, it brings chances to adjust.

I know the frustration of having everything
You say read into, I do!
Because now I realize what I have, it's you!
You won't fade away if I put that blasted hammer down
For a moments rest and feel the calm with you.

Sleepless Dream Window

Wait for silent, invisible feelings to form.
Let things slip into the unreachable.
Worry doesn't take your mind since
Nothing can ever really vanish.
Instead it just slowly fades in and out.

Be the one who remains unrecognizably strong.
Be the one who dares to know.
Diversity, is it oppression against one another?

Forgiveness toils through caverns,
Moss and earth blend, moisten and spread together
along the walls, always will there be walls.

New experiences with morals overdue.
Who will reach out and grasp them?
As they shine like the diamonds of a wedding.

Collide with the invisible oppression.
It was silent before the interception between you.
Silently cry another invisible tear
from the fears harboured within.

Smile

No words can help
My aching heart now.
Things have been good,
But I still wonder how I'll survive,
Without your eyes and smile.

The quest of life
was answered for me with you.
But I'm told it's not free.
Losing you, I know. So what can I do?

Stop the panic,
Hold off on the words,
I'm telling myself.
Just fly fast through work.
Making as much as I can,
It's all entirely for you.

Every day that goes by,
Is another day I fall further,
Into your love and into your enchantment over me.
I hope there's a place in your mind,
For my face, for my smile and eye's.

Preserving your river love,
Never getting enough,
If it's to be held off baby,
Then don't worry.
I won't go crazy; just turn to granite inside.
So look my way and smile, for me!?

The Gathering

Just not happy with reality,
There is a need to break free.
I keep telling myself to move without thought.
The second is forever the chain,
Willingness to break and follow is the ball.

Give me the hack saw,
Standing here and following a zombie groove
is so much better than sitting and reflecting.
Dim the lights, I love the moon;
Simulate the moon.

In lesser words a gathering will whisper,
"Togetherness will make the underground dreams,
Which always falls into the piranha infested flow
Of the mainstream."

I would love to bring something terrible,
To something beautiful.
Hear all willows with their whispers (the gathering).
Bazaarness will fill every possible crack and crevice,
That can and does exist within all that remains in the world.

Beware of the trees,
For their tangled twisted arms reach for thee.
Break and burn,
And they will all fall in martyr defense.

Now, in the moment in which you topple,
Upon the dirt, laying in the puddle.
There will be no air for your lungs,
And still none will care.
No one cares even if you're young and chopped down from all angles.

The Foolish Runaway King

Deep within his mind,
There are countless regrets.
Always a willingness to make peace with others;
Especially the ones that should remain out of reach.

The battle inside his head will probably never rest,
For the memories will forever sail in the wind.
Just like the flags upon the polls of his battalion ships.

Sinking those ships, the ambush brings them down.
Crying and mistaking and floundering wash up over all his troops.
Now, left an embarrassed man, he wonders what the new year
To come will bring him.

Will there be any new lands conquered?
Or just old ones lost with pain
as they are taken and in turn, forgotten.

So he'll sit here upon his now empty throne and try to
Conjure his rebuilt troops at his enemies' castle.
And again, his willingness and love for peace,
Will overpower his victory.

Creation of Government and False Freedom

New beginnings echo visions,
Of better beautiful places and
Deeper inner strength.

Built in focus is never
always present with what you want to do.
It's hard to take the jump,
When you want the sex so much when you were a child.

They say it's all found in youth.
The rest of your life is spent trying to get there.
First word association really killed it all for everyone.
I just don't know what we're doing.
God gave us to choice to define our own bible,
Our own agenda.
But who knows what the main moral will be?

Politicians try to be mentors,
Try to be companions and parents…
Government!

Where I Fit in

You're so brilliant, I'm so shallow,
I'm drowning in
the puddles under your feet.

Sun always graces your eyes,
Do the questions ever stop?
When I look there can be seen,
Nothing but the bottom of your soul.
I guess this is my sky, sun and moon.

One wrong word,
And you're walking over me.
Never forgetting what was done,
As you stomp away.

Days drift by,
These wounded trampled wings never seem to heal.
So slowly life exists,
As we're so much farther and uglier from the truth.

I just want to see the picture,
You see, all of God's creations.
They're all precious,
They all hold a piece of the key to truth and heaven.

To know where I fit in with them,
In that picture.
To know what piece of the key I am.
Would it reveal my place in heaven?
Maybe up to your level even?

Faster Than the Eye 2: Don't Stop

Here in the night,
Do you feel the pinch?
Of our leeching society.

Is there weak places
far inside your eaten body?
"Oh, how they fed off my advantage."

Don't stop the tears,
When the last penny's gone.
Don't stop the tears,
When your strength collapses.
And don't stop the tears,
When the memories flood back.
Don't let failure defeat or zombiefy you...
Defy them.

Goodbye, My Son

Here in the streets,
Enduring the rain.
I feel a heavy burden resting on my head.

Traveling from each place
to the next like a rebel messenger.
This could never be crazier.

Don't you feel the cotton brush touch
from the hands of death.
I'll stay far from all dark shadows.

Now instantly through more blurry uncertainty,
It all happens again.
I meet the challenger.

I feel pain slowly just before death slips
through these skies above me.
"Goodbye, my son" you bid.
Regret seeps through these skies;
As I go along with the rivers that wash from me.
"Just goodbye, my son".

Call of Homeland

Tension grips me,
Leaves a burning fire within.
Only a short time till I am ready for work,
Only a short time since that bottle of malice has departed.

It's not easy with all of this openness.
Emotions in a world of capitalized approach...
You see it transform to prey,
You see softness die under the predators.

Home beckons hard,
My life story is experienced
and safety forever my desired alley.

In a city where imagination and sincerity are extinct
reason and chances fly from the window.

So here again in open cold air,
Water trails down as I feel the pain.
When can the craziness end for me?
How long until home sets me free?

Unlikely Desire

A million miles fast,
Unthought-of magnificent heights.
Bigger and larger than ever before,
But it brings to me an uncontrollable craving
for knowledge and power.

Reoccurring bursts of panic and rage subside,
To hints at total acceptance of fate.
This sudden quietness and stillness;
I really want it to stay and will participate to achieve…
But how much and long will it take?

Entire inclusion of mindset,
No bigger confusion shows evident.
Desires I will defend and get anyway though.

So what else could I say?
All these points of control are slowing me down.
Maybe you'd like to help.
Where should you start? What do you really want?

Needed Sanctuary

Take on the weight,
Of everybody's conscience.
Guilty secrets keep you soothing others.

It has been a long damn road,
Cut loose tonight.
Is there possibility you'd care to hear my story?
And cut loose tonight?

Right through this wall we could break!
In the midst of commotion,
There is sanctuary.
Would you go there with me?

Uplifted

Alone with thoughts,
Again those stones slide.
Sun is blocked from sight and
Continuously the path is travelled.

I'm not one for time,
Up from the ground a stake sits.
Whichever angle its shadow reaches;
Whichever stones are washed once
more as the waves retreat.

Beneath thick boughs,
Dim brown and green lead me to roadside.
Footprints, filled with water,
Lead in both directions.

And what have I brought from this exploration?
Every colour of the sky shines so beautifully
As a bird is uplifted from under those
green sheltering trees by the wind,
carried out over the waves and
away from wear and time.

An Ugly Skies A Beautiful Farewell

They say all of the things that haunt you,
Are those that which you have suffered from.
They are things you detest,
They are things you grow to like.

Here in the heart,
My fears and desires go hand in hand.
Better judgement rules the land,
No safe haven or time from its cold iron grip.

I could never share with anyone,
The things, objects and imagery of my thoughts and memories.
Too strong for my control,
Yet I wonder how I got away from my past with my soul.

I turn from these storms with thorns and pins
in my sides, in my heart.
Maybe you could lead my mind,
Lead my eyes too! Lead my spirit to the sky.

Help me fit each rolling,
Fluffy cloud with a different thorn.
And each colour with a pin.

How grand would it be,
To see a sky of ghosts,
ugly people and haunting memories…
Just sail away from here,
For good.

Lord, I Know I Want the Light

Lord I know, oh Lord I know.
It's never the same as you,
No matter what I could ever say or do.

Changes are different from each other,
Each time the conditions change.
I'd hate to think I have a clue.
Because everything I want cannot be reached.
I feel so smothered and it's all so strange;
For your love tells me my maps are miscalculated!

The things I once indulged in,
I now repel from.
Pathways are shifting all about.
I know it's for the better but
I cannot figure my way out.

And Lord I know,
Oh Lord I know I've got to hang on,
Just until the end.
I have to figure out what's wrong.

Your helping hand I long for.
Lead me;
For oh Lord I know I want the light.

Standing Before Oblivion

I don't want to be obvious,
Defying you seems like walking into oblivion.
It takes so much just to make a stand,
God I'm entirely lost.

What's my problem? What's my disease?
Seems like I'm trying to please everyone but myself.

So should I collapse and go back on my word?
Maybe I could finish the plan.
Stick to my guns and head homeward.

It takes so much just to make a stand.
Feels like I'm at the edge leading into oblivion
as this waltz continues on.

...God, I'm entirely lost.

Searching and Determined

…And there was a time,
When I could look to the sky.
I would feel the moon hit these eyes
Strong enough to stir some passion.

But now I'm so far away,
From that long gone day,
When this mystery started to matter to me.

So who are you to rightly say
that what I see isn't good enough for me?
And it's all so much better for you now,
You know what it was that haunted me.
The rain feels so much warmer,
And the dark shadows no longer cross your path.

But that's okay really.
It's just more to watch at the corner of my eyes.
Another reason to pray to the skies
As another shadow fills my sights.

As The Truth Just Comes Ringing Out

I suppose this cause is lost,
In front of you: oh how must I be?
Do I shine with the brilliance of individualism and oneness,
Or is there a further hatred for my heart?

What would it be,
If all the little pieces suddenly came together,
In this crazy screwed up life and fit?
Do you know what it's like to really want?

And maybe I do deserve all the blame,
I mean, in life, who ever really knows what they're doing right?
But I'll just speak from this old heart,
Yet I simply can't seem to find a way to concede.

There always seems to be resistance coming from myself,
Never is there a sense of achievement or defeat.
Maybe limbo can't go the distance,
I'm telling you it feels like nothing at all!
And that's every clue I have.

Have imagination and imagine.
Let it speak with ringing magical mystical words.
Hear your own singing echoing voice,
As the truth just comes ringing out.

The Fool's Full Circle

You are the familiar surface which I love so.
These new strides, the new beginnings!
That old colour, that old ending.

White washed walls, shape shifted walls.
Bigger and better diamonds, years set back.
Perhaps I could build a fence,
With the bones of every skeleton in my closet.
Perhaps I could hope, pray and feebly attempt,
To keep the haunting memories, demons
and knives from my back.

I believe, like most, some sins help protect.
White lies are related to exceptions.
Nothing is total occurrence, only partial
(no matter the frequency large or small).

So maybe for every time I spat upon the Lord,
I was really nailing another picket to the fence
of bones that will keep me safe.
That will establish my sanctuary.

Now here at these shape shifted white washed walls I will gaze.
Upon the jewels and riches which I possess.
These I will use to buy the needed things of every soul,
Which I have locked away in my closet.
Each a possible chance to use for my ascension
to that place which is above.

Then once I have paid my sinful debts,
I will once again be holding the paint and brush in my hand.
I will be staring at the red running dripping walls.
These tell-all running, dripping, inescapable walls.

Deep Inside My Mind

I can't seem to escape from all
of the fears that are deep inside my mind.

Manifested hurts just come
springing out from your mouth.
I guess things would have been free
and rich for you if we would have
trekked to the crossroads and gave in.

But now here we are instead.
Amongst countless future dreams;
That are all pinned to the wall.
Far into the night I will always hear your call
deep inside my mind.

I will search and cry for always.
I will kiss and chase you to the end always.
When I am left to guess what is remaining for me
I will, in that moment, see your face always.
Deep inside my mind I love and fear you.

Confidence in Devotion

Burning flame, charred remains and a soul with miles.
Countless mistakes, moments of hate and
oh those tears in your eyes.

So baby maybe you're not the one for me oh no
and baby just maybe you're the only one who can save me.

I fear the approach of insane emotions,
I can only promise my utmost devotion.
You set it all off in me,
Oh how can this ever not be?

Just look in my eyes, see the flame
and believe me when I say that you fit me perfectly.
Take my words, look in my eyes
and there you'll see the charred dead remains of my fears.
Remember these flames which arise.
Let them guide you.

Nowhere

Here in the golden skies
reality rules surreal.
You cannot escape forever;
Ever under your own control.

So go ahead and blame
everything and everyone,
When your image is shattered.
I guess all the complications,
Expectations and distractions is becoming your damnation.

Far above this earth,
Your soul lingers.
Never good enough
To be upheld as positive.
Never respected even close
to the point of being feared.

So here the urge to rule withdraws
and betrays you (as you feared it would).
The urge…. the withdrawal.
Takes you down, keeps you out,
Fills your mind, absorbs control.
Keeps you out, fills your mind,
Absorbs control; takes you down.
Caught in between; Damned both ways.

Life's Journey: A Sequel from Lost to Love: Pt. 1
Misled (By Following Hindsight)

Everything, at times, seems to spiral out of resemblance.
I gain no satisfaction out of trying to use my hindsight.

All of the tiny articles and pleasantries I enjoy,
Evasively creep away to leave my life far from memorable
and all together vague.

Searching and looking I've inched my way to the very outer limits.
Not a damn thing have I recollected.
They've all vanished; there are no pieces around.

In a nutshell life is breath.
It is beat of the heart,
With that old humbleness too.
I spend the remainder of it searching for those articles
and pleasantries of years past then suddenly I realize,
I'm not so close to you anymore.

Part 2: Letting Go (Back to You)

Now at my back the hard cold stone walls
cut my journey down.
Inside this ring nothing can be found,
Nothing can get in!

My past, I adulated… imploringly too.
Now at the brink I can see there is only
one thing for me to do.
Scale the wall.

Turn my back on all of the people
inside this ring of memories.
Let go of past glories,
Set the present free to rise, to transcend!
These are the pieces,
They are the clues I have searched for.

In hand they bring me to walls top.
I will not look back but jump off.
Into your arms I pour my love back to you.

Letting go and moving on I weep over your shoulder.
Wishing we had back all of the time I wasted.

Part 3: Moving On Together

Letting go of me, you pull from your pocket
A piece of chalk.
Across the wall you triumphantly write
"Conquered".

There is a cloudless sky,
For you and I oh yes.
Our love encircles and holds us both as one.

I feel your heart beating.
I smell how you taste,
And shiver at your crazy, wonderful flavor.

Believe me, trust me,
I have searched for a more profound meaning.
Only to realize that going forward,
Going up is the one way to never lose who you are.
Baby, you are the biggest of me.
We are free now and forever more.

Loving the Ground You're On

Do these morals really rule so high?
This life, this love I have so good
and so true is it what you are looking for too?

Dear friend, things go wrong in life,
Sometimes that oak snaps to the fury of the wind.
Now are you going to put your own hate filled
meaning in my words?
Instead, why can't we all just wish each other well?

Forgive me if I tend to speak
of serious matters and things that are not
pleasurable to your fun.
It bottles up in me,
I speak to no one of the matters inside,
Sometimes the top bursts open,
Sometimes I break under the stress of all the issues.
Everything, everyone has its time.

But I would gladly strain against the pain
and fall into the fire instead of on you my friend.
I wish you all the luck in the end,
I hope you're doing the same for me.
I love my place in life,
This hilltop is the only place I have been,
Right here for me is the only place I want to be.

360 Degrees

Stemming from my past
are the identity pieces which make me up today.
All of the urges and sins I am
come from yesterday.

I was told by many people
about the personal moods we feel towards ourselves;
Turns out they show their severity and effects on us.

To be contained and so specific within such a boundless world.
Self-withdrawn and tunnel eyes so long, deep and black
you'd think yourself inanimate.
Where is the connection? Where is my influence?

So I'll march through the streets.
Greeting all of the people whom I meet.
Praying on wounded and swollen knees,
That I'll always keep my ability to move 360 degrees.
So I may fulfill my purpose.

Please Don't Go

This cover is blown,
Down falls confidence and victory.
All that remains at all for me to give,
All that is left to want from me is the truth.

No trust for me.
I'm the one way street to hell.
Unwanted, unremembered.
In life totally far from being an influence,
In death absolutely forgotten.

Try so hard,
Always sound exactly the same.
Nothing ever seems to change or grow.
Every moment feels like an unwinnable game.

Who was it that decided I was too happy?
I am me, you are you.
what did I do?
Nothing is ever 100 percent,
But there's no balance flowing my way.

So for sure I need help,
A person to call "Companion!"
I miss you so.
Please don't go.

Outside of Eden

Work through the world and give us a sign!
Grab our imagination and with it,
strike your fear and power into our hearts.

There's a solid black line,
that none must dare to cross.
Whoa to those that tread its farthest side,
for over there, on the other side,
our imagination runs wild against us.

Flames scorch and burn
all the temples and civilizations of time.
Those foolish ones ate that apple
and swallowed their banishment.

So in that sentencing we are here on the outside of Eden.
We too choose either to eat our piece of the
forbidden fruit or to follow along as best we can.
In that garden lives honour and peaceful truth
and so to it our journey is made to head.

Go With Your People

What was it that we wanted?
What was it that you brought?
What was it that I had?
What is this that we now seem to have?

Never have I thought
that you have all of the answers.
Never have I thought
that I have none.

But to be fair and honest then;
What was and what is wrong with everything
we now have?
Where is the difference from 'that which is good'
and that which you repel from?

Understand your opinion is you, not fact.
So do not beat me down.
I am good for me, people like me.
You are good for you, people like you.
Go with your people, I will with mine.

Being Free and Alone

It's hard to keep the faith,
When everyone around instills that fear into you.
It's difficult to let go,
When your own mind is the enemy.

At night, when you walk through forests.
Does your mind bring forth a merging
of memory, imagination and fantasy?
Well does it bring those things but
in the form of sweat and shadows?

I meet new faces in new places and hope
to shift to reinforced steel that is
moulded around control-and-contentment.
Truth is a mix of something tainted and something pure…
No chance of molecules and particles bonding at all.

Yes, there was a time when this river ran,
raged under storm clouds and opened up and poured forth.
Debris washed away in a cleansing of the forest.
The nightly air (with its sorrow and isolation)
would help me let go.
You see, I welcomed it for its gift of freedom to me.

It's not so much for what I don't have,
It's actually the things that I do which hurt and worry me.
So, how do I let go?

Ignorance in the Face of Allegiance

Feel the fears all around you. Why do you run? Why do you hide? In the end, everyone dies. Everything fades. All is lost. You seek what you cannot find, you desire the things you already have. There may never be an answer for you but still here you are for all to see….. How can this be?

Existence within core definition,
All those who hate one another who are different.
You don't understand, so you'll kill for thrill!
You don't understand, so you'll kill for thrill!
What is your disease? What is your cause?
What is your needed answer? What are your responsibilities?

So here we go again within the walls of our minds. No one seems to understand, no one seems to find the things they want. The ways we need. All the focused young, imagination-life crashed was yanked and faded away.

Enemies within bliss,
Ignorance in the face of blood and damage.
Lost causes and miscalculated morals.
Communication fading,
Monsters rising.
Communication disappearance,
Monsters conquering.

Everyone seems to preach alliance, yet still they all evoke the fears themselves! What have we done? Where have we gone wrong?

Social Illusions

Drunk environment, swaying walls and thoughts of
all of the things that I do not have; that I dream and long so hard for.
Where I have been mistaken? Where have I devastated my groundings this much?
Self-pity is a dangerous game, just like forsaking your roots.

Where you came from is exactly what's there in that mirror before you.
Where you go is just a display of its influence over you.
So tell me wise one,
Are they strong or are they weak?
So tell me wise one,
Are they right or are they a real dose?

So sit and listen, throw it all away.
So sit and listen, fade down dark and fill with dismay.
Relax back and justify.
Relax back and watch suicide before your eyes.
Your crying, begging, swollen eyes.

Pride Damages

Disconnection, rejection, isolation.
Desecration, underestimation.
And every other gift we get from life's friendly foes.

Guaranteed its felt by them too, who push it on; every day is a struggle!
Yes it would help if I was there.
I feel your suffering losses.

I hear your voice inside my mind.
I hold on to help… but you've been cast out.
Can't change things with a corpse,
And so the end result dances illusively.

I got this pain along the side of my head.
Yearning for a migraine even though I know it's this
painful connection to you.

Fears are all around,
Nothing can be found of your heart,
I think it all got lost at the start.
This pain, oh it begins to hurt now.

I'm feeling what you've left for me.
This disconnection, rejection, isolation.
Desecration, underestimation.
I'm feeling you go through it too.

These make up the great big obstacles that's in our way.
Change my pride to bring this to a rightful end.
Because who are you and what's my crime?
Hurry up and answer, since underneath the orange sky
fate has all but died.

Troubled

Questions rumble to answers,
Statements and relations.
Procrastinate every single emotion away,
Be so self-withdrawn,
Be so full of vengeance.

I can't take this tension,
Seams tear and ridges crack.
Feeling through and through
as I force down on this tension.
Seeing myself appearing to crack
as it tears my heart apart.

Forget all this heartache.
Walk, finally, among every stranger.
I seem to be damning myself as
It's happening around me; trouble!

I can't seem to escape it.... Trouble.
I'm feeling troubled down through.

Surviving Melancholy

You see me looking meticulously at world, at you!
Picking out all of the small things,
Concentrating on each tiny detail;
Every one individually.

Each an everlasting moment of melancholy soul,
Melancholy spirit.
Recorded facts.
The analytical eyes have cast their judging gaze and have tried!

I see you as very relaxed and on edge inside.
Storing energy for something that, no doubt, has to do with pride.
Everywhere, everything is merged together; one outcome,
One object to really lose it all over.

Oh yes, all of the objects of your mind are prodigies.
Enigmas to their very own paradoxes of circumstances.
All follow a code to One Outcome.
There is no individuality,
Soul and spirit drift away.
In time all things of control change,
eventually emoting to melancholy in the end.

So tell me am I stupid for focusing
on every detail individually?
I keep my things apart,
I do not merge.
This way I have more things to grasp when I fall!

Now in eternal flowing time,
The facts will show when we died
and from what and it will show how we felt.

Visions In Your Eyes

Visions in your eyes,
Things on your mind,
It seems to you that it's just not there.

People who care and who dare to go
where you need them to be the most.
So just finally break down for once in
your life; opportunity is best friends
with first impression… it only comes once.
It's always in your hands by the right of choices.
Those foolish, cold, unforgiving,
unchanging, heartless choices.

No there is no blame because to me it's not a game.
Competition is hated and painted red.
Experience is supreme
and only honest care will ever salvage us
before we are all eventually dead.

However, although all of this is now said.
Watching you intently I can see a flicker
of those visions in your eyes
and of those things on your mind.
I hope that I'm standing in your vision
when you look around for another person for compassion.

Because for all of the pain you feel,
I feel it too! And for what you went through I did, too.
And if I'm wrong then just let me get
to know you now.

No Toys Nor Tests

My mind is so twisted,
Sometimes I think maybe the end is better.
How do I know what I'll do before
the morning light comes in to burn my eyes?
It puts everything under the veil of such
wicked disguise.

Now I made a mistake, one that kept you up late.
Now I'm hoping there's still the familiarity here for me.

Don't yell trust because that old trick is old with rust.
I just couldn't control the crazy feeling you give me.
Whisper "It's okay, just not again."
That would win my heart in the end of this,
I need to know now if you're forgiving to me.

No this is not a test I'm not like the rest.
I don't toy with the heart, it's so hard to put back together
once it's been broken apart, broken apart, broken apart....
Well not by me.

Playing With Contempt

I never know where to go or what to do!
Advice and directions are no good;
Read a full description of the movie before watching!?
I'm here staring back at you...
Only two feet away distant oh unreachable horizon.

My head has always gotten the better of me.
It's makes you read into me, me into you.
It's makes me read into you, you into me!
What can I do? Everything I fear is slowly creeping
inside my conscience!
These walls submerged within are far stronger
than my grit and strength ever expected them to be.
God, karma, somebody help?!

Zero participation I would have given
to that deadly game of hide my answers,
I never would have played
if it meant that nobody understands me
for the rest of my days.
These walls submerged within,
Your only against my touch now dear horizon.
I won't play that damn game of hide the pain.
Now nobody understands me, saying I'm too hard to get.
Now I'm all alone again, cold bricks and dried cement
against my palms and face.

Golden Ocean Clouds

Soft but sharp,
Deep and strong,
Something that can last oh so long.

After it has died and all of us have lied,
we'll have a chance to live our visions,
and make decisions that show, in the end,
what we've reached for.
So stand and sway in the winds which may
blow against you.
Having become turned so indifferent
to what you really have.

It's not that bad, really it's easy.
Going back at this point isn't appealing.
But from here I can watch golden ocean clouds,
Sailing high in and throughout the skies with
the winds of change.

Me Leader

Here in another day, a different way to fall down
Into the cracks where nothing seems to be flowing.
Inescapable, unclimable walls all around,
When will the exit become clear?

Along the narrowing path where these walls leave only
enough space between for my foot to frantically walk,
I can feel the surging boiling touch of panic at my throat.

Slipping on through to the other side,
Where shadows lurk in darkness.
Down under I can feel them grasping now;
I'm breathless!

Under to the top looking down below.
I can see myself throwing me down that hole.
Every night I'm my own master.
The pilot of this flight of light and shadows.
Ups and downs, ins and outs, highs and lows
of the inescapable caverns of life.

Cowherds

Ball of cobwebs and lies,
words are the spiders trail.
Life's current forms me, you
and everybody doomed into
some directed, inspired faith.
But of what?

Actions is the here and now.
Words are from everywhere.
Feelings and emotions the past and present.

We do where, what we can.
Faster than trust.
Knowing of what made us.

Yet down along that river,
Bobbing, wet and coughing.
Somebody collided with the cobwebs.
Thought of a way to preserve their lust for life even more
and ended drained of their blood.

In the web, along the river in
which they acted to jump towards.
They were trying to escape fear.

Invaluable Dreams of Love

Glimmering diamonds, their eye catching
saving grace; sand and mud around it.
The contrast possessed by walls
of stone around him.

In such a dark, he gazes outward to his nightly sky.
With so many a number of glimmering stars
and wishes edging the tip of tongue now.
Brought back into the days of time with you.

Up against his heart burning in his belly.
A desire of fire so intense it's scary now.
Flooding back, soaked and yet unknown to be drowned.

That creature of ringing open air's here now.
Sharp pains shot through his head
as anticipation merged with realization.
It was there for him that control seeped out and vanished.
This moment held imagination for him instead.
This he realized while crouched down,
Sobbing from relief against his heart
with yours in his.

Dangerous Situations, Dangerous Games

Dangerous situations, dangerous games. Little morsels run down the nose, drip off and land past the edge of repair. The heat inside and out forces it down, you're sweating now. Way into the thickest of forest the chase led you. Overgrown and oh so small these droplets of blood appear, cold iron grip around the crucifix sword. To die cold, damp and lead astray not today there is faith keeping weapon strong. Inquisitive jolts smoke the head, burnt hair! Would you care, no you're just an empty a space of void; one of the demons, a shadow shape of infinite hate and appearing as something less than invisible, as the closest to nothingness that can be! Down you walk along the dried graveyard river bed. Slimy rocks and mud under your feet and a void where your heart should be. Up to the sketchy gray rolling, full moonlit cloudy sky, you pray and cry and cry "This is a dangerous situation, a dangerous game! So I will pass this shadowsoul on to the other side. Killing every emotion deep down, I must now outlive the family from whence I came... I will overcome!"

Seekers

Along the street he would walk steady paced into the next hour; he never even at all talked. There was an intent that burned with some power and the sky was already observed by him. Confessing and informing of how it was always something to be learned, always showing something imaginative and whimsical in character. Following that burning orange flame, he felt it inside and out; oh how intense! Parsed lips and a full mind of discern; later they would be with their passion tonight.

He longed for the warmth of her thighs and soft skin, she longed for the strength of his arms around her. His chest, her breast, their love... never enough! This was the fire within the cavern of steady foot upon cement where dropped the sweat. Black trench coat concealing it all to boots and around, in and all about and far into the air, where he felt a tingling energy of heat very bazaar. Looked about and saw her standing there, under the red traffic light at the paved crossroads. She looked finally to the thought from her mind, the face held by her memory and imagination. So profound in character they seemed to each other.

Fascination, determination of love and longing for lust, "These are all of the things that I have, that I've come to know I need. All I rightfully and understandingly want with these words are rested feet and long forgotten skies of loneliness." They whispered tenderly together as they found safe haven escape within each other.

Meaning vs Man

I feel like I have a shadow for a soul
and a million days gone on alone.
Steady thinking to myself of the meaning
in any of this.

Just where did the hate seep in?
My pokes couldn't have been as bad as that.
Well now my friend just close your eyes
to the memories of you robbing me.

Anything you want to believe, you can lead yourself to believe.
Don't ever forget, you never let me forget it's affected by your opinion.
Water to music, sustenance to wind.
Cool whispering trickles from the water's
as I often fretted over this.

So down along the bend in this path,
Just where the walking trail comes level with the water.
We'd all best be careful of where the soil is no longer.
Sinking sand there so know your ground!

Finally the thought appears to me,
Reflected in the water.
It's just like they said,
"It's not the artist that matters but the art."

Missing the Colours by Looking Into Them

Opinions and details sail into the wind.
It casts a song, it sings with the trees.
A child feels the goose bumps and coolness against skin,
Another leaf falls down before him.

Just what these reflections show,
It's sitting in rippling mirror.
Trying so very hard and far,
Only to ever see what it was they knew.

So down heavy burden air comes, settles and burns his face.
Pride inside swells to rebirth of rage.
Sometimes people plan to exterminate sin.
Too bad for those sitting leaves,
Is it the fault of the tree that they die?

Where could death be credited and
just what is it that makes it so bad?

Shades of grey never catch his eyes;
Into the puddle water now.
Only thing seen are the leaves that fall.

So look past the muddy floor of that green topped ocean,
And not onto the colours that surround the vessel representing
life which is sailing in that little pool.
So look past any relatable emotion or thought,
Only to register a leaf.

Shadowsouls

Some people get their esteem at the expense of others,
oh poor wretch, lying still in the stress swamp of life.
Innocence took out all our vengeance,
still night air brings the heat and sweat
through our hair with little regard and care.

Sometimes a moment strikes me,
venting is a word I will always change on.
Personal opinion cracks at the base,
having it's cement poured and moulded many years ago.

This terribly, shockingly afraid feeling faded.
Crying eyes saw all the colours of life shining in and
something strange drained out.
I still hear it calling sometimes,
at the graveyard along the road of…
never appeared to…
and I tried…
but nothing ever came to be.

So where were you when we wandered off?
Memories sailing away over the edge of the world,
lost when carried inside the space
of your old-world-fashioned mind.

I remember how I felt about his death.
Oh, it hurt so bad; I was terribly, shockingly afraid.
Crying saw all the colours of life shining in and
something strange drained out.
I still hear it calling sometimes.

You're Out of Sight While Standing Beside Me

Seeping, grinding, mismatched understanding.
Knowledge and treason in every word we profess.
Up straight at the distant orange horizon,
we now echo in unison, "Our eyes... see now!"

Never go back and read, but forge ahead
down through the mud as you dig your path,
focus on the forms, something of worth.
Those birds fluttering calling, crying and
easing our thoughtrains.

Stop along the cobblestone sidewalk,
bathing in the fashioned, ornamented street lights.
To fly away into the sunset and forget,
to enter tomorrow with true first impression,
memory turning from the past.
I thought we were both standing atop the same pillar, you and I,
when I said I wanted to enter tomorrow without any of those memories.

My Own Conspiring Mind

Drifting all throughout the air and waves,
people with their smiles and dizzy haze.
Nothing deeper than midnight air,
so long and lonely and busy with thought
we think all is all but lost.

So take a walk, down the trail,
away from the entire world and you will fail
to see the opportunity in this moment
because the peace will settle the realizing voice within.

The twisted tangled arms of trees reaching for the sky,
Now hold and embrace their song.
Rustling and swaying, they are the sight and dance for my eyes,
easing my questions of "Why?"
My millions of questions all worded "Why?"

Up to the grey-scattered, drifting clouds,
alit by the moon which hangs so low.
I see the birds sail across this picture,
they land in the song and sway along with the twisted arms.

From the skies these birds land in the trees, messengers to lungs,
who have summoned the bland, black, countless murder.
Run and I stumble under weary feet,
But beaks and crowing are much more than I can take,
I'm growing weak, swimming in the red river.

They peck and they tear at my mind when I despair.
Screaming and sweating I awake from slumber
seeing that I did not stumble.
Here, alone with my thoughts, which I sought an escape from
with my sleep…but my mind summons the dreams…
The environments of bland, black murder,
my screams feed him…
My fear, our fear. We all know it well.

Masks and Melancholy

Wading through the seaside water,
It's up to my chest… neck, with the rolling waves.
All around me is water gold.
Sky's wearing his pastel coloured coat again.

I shed a tear in this ocean and feel a little better to never know just where it landed.
Looking down, I see my rippling reflection and grow heavier.

Up, out and to the beach and sand, trekking for miles and miles.
The footprints are washed away.

And I think to myself, "Is it just this?
Day after day with this tingling sensation of pain
that numbs all my senses
and leaves me never knowing from where I've come or how I feel?"

This mask of pain I wish I could remove it long enough
to know if I should throw it away or use it against the sharks of the day
and the vultures of the night.

Do I need cover? Burden kept to deflect further burden.
Collapsing on the beach leaving the imprint of a fallen one.
Feels so melancholy and I'm drained further, hurting further.
The hope that is day after day with no better heights or depths
than the other, slips further away.

I wish this mask would reach and cover my mind,
to leave all this pain and stalling melancholy so very far behind.
I think this to myself as I wade through the water
and shed more wretched tears.
"Oh God, I wish I was so much more numb than this."

Dying Passion Sanctuary

Restraint clawing at all edges of reality;
Observing a loss of image upon some old man's canvas.
Jolts and nervous twitches sail away time;
Yes oh always facing the day that one!

We all remember well the rain on that cloudy night,
When he realized nothing is what his paintings had become.
His dream fading past the edges of reality,
fantasy lost into toiling discouragement.

Loss of empathy filled his eyes,
where the heavy grey ruled the skies,
and the rain brought on the shivers,
and the cold, constant, recognizing, unrelenting indifference.

God, My Conqueror

Cool goosebumps spreading across the skin.
Cool neon, navy blue sky
etching itself into soul.

Hoping eyes, remembering all the
details within you.
While continuing to defeat and hold the enemies;
(keeping hope alive).

Upon the day that battle is won,
My father, you will walk with me,
With your ever understanding grace
that shall instil peace into my heart.

We will journey in love together,
until the night falls all around.
The thoughts of the past shall be wiped away,
from this sanctuary we will have.
I shall tremble with joy,
whenever I hear words
from your mouth.

Revolution for Flaming Desire

Park bench along the littered street.
Wide paved sidewalks and people to meet,
to greet with talk of implications and freedoms.
Some of movement and communication,
others found in hesitation and thoughts that sail out of your head.

Idle chat attaching straight into you.
Tighten your grasp on the edge,
while the cool wind breeze pushes,
and tugs out and away the resistance.

Now look up over shoulder into distant sky,
take hold of this revolution.
Feel burning flames within… some power.
Jump, push past, run down the street.

Paying no heed to the people or to whom you could meet and relate.
Overrunning the boundaries and automatic defences.
Feel the revolution burning through all of your senses
with its flame of desire.

Clenching your eyes so tight,
envisioning the sanctuary you have waiting ahead.
Truly the only one of its kind…
A place of solace and possibilities for you.

Co-operations Possibilities

Feels as though everything has come together;
Bursting upon collision.
Chilled skin shivering in unison with
chattering teeth.
No place appears free to me; not one!

Main streets of our lives,
fear seeps all through.
Street lamps remain as the
solid constant entity, the light
and oh that light from above.

Past events where time and place,
and sometimes even atmosphere treated each other with a dignity.
It was solid and constant,
and no one along all the roadsides anywhere,
or anyone amongst those clouds ever missed it,
or ever let their hope for it die.

Some jogged along the streets and looked in every direction for it.
Others ran frantically, turning over trash cans
and peering into large soaked cardboard boxes.
The smart ones created it with each other;
they knew the value of co-operation.

The Electronic Impression

Drifting just about a foot or so,
Old still unconnected wires of old and new
(which were started from both ends).

Within a crevice lay remains,
and you find a link to the spiritual realm here!
Come lay down your batteries,
abandon the electricity for a moment
and mourn the loss.

Boulders forming defences.
Horseless chariots of plastic, steel, metal and smoke;
Oh killing smoke.
Beware the moose dear navigator of
destinationless journey.

Up and about to move beyond,
rising forth is the oppressed beast.
Terrified and farther than brink driven,
to the sprawling ominous mountains
It moves; gateway to the beyond.

Growing slowly but set in plastic stone.
Our circuits programmed by imagination killers
who possess the fast knowledge that in the old,
slower world...
There was time to see the earth alive.
Poor apparent fate; world disappearing in fact.

Freedom by Foot

Outside and in there's
long, smooth surfaces, angles, colours;
feel those textures, surfaces and materials!
Doors securely shut and thrown open.

Tingling, sweet scented air,
No longer or stronger desired aroma brings me closer.
Plans and light beneath oil thick darkness,
dying animal instinct stares.

Allure rushing pullingly and fadedly leading,
Perhaps to the rising North with rolling white winds
or straight ahead with the town
snd it's better access to more out in the open defences.

Back from up my street I remain,
Seeing and hearing the calling and images of these presences.
Rolling tires pulls my strength out;
Exploring by foot keeps it up.
Don't you, wouldn't anyone feel
such a free, healing aspect of this life
from a slow, self-controlled strengthening
method as this?

The Beach of Broken Emotions

Building and welling within,
crying calling raging voices tear and rip.
Same old vocabulary… words.
Unchanged options… actions, movements.

It's easy for that polar bear to seem indignant,
when torn away from home and kept in the cages.
The trainers ask too much from it, it can't understand
human word commands as well as you try to force it.

Times in the evening, the burning grows until on this day
it broke out and away.
Following the caressing call of the waves,
out over rippling water's surface it tries to run,
only deeper as it swims and is shot.
Can you hear that final roaring from over there in the red water?
Night shows it wasting down to ashes.
So the morning brings flowers to the grave of the bear,
shot down when tried for freedom from the cage;
To a much bigger cage.

In the city things are numb with temptation and convenience.
So alone and miserable, but unbothered beliefs lay there.
I don't think hell is completely full of evil, vile ones,
So many stones are thrown down on the beach.
This boy is only looking for smooth,
saucer-like rocks… no others.

So the rock collection fills a large bucket now
for skipping stones along the water.
His favourite place to feel in tune with the world.
But what of those still trapped in that zoo?
I don't think there is a point to this poem,
just like there is no point to capturing anything inside a cage.
It's easy to seem so small and little,
when the disrespect piled on you,
is over shot and leaves you shouting to be understood.

Little boy skips a last stone,
it bounces once for all the friends he's ever known.
Ran away from home because Mommy and Daddy
are conformists just like the door man to heaven.
He whispers this through determination to be his own
to his dead fury friend beneath the beautiful flowers
on the beach of broken emotions.

Cannibal Love

Lying in bed picking, licking
sliding hands across this chest and thighs.
Far below under these skies a beauty
pushes harder than ever before to believe.

So you fade away into the night,
no one brings a tolerance or truth.
Fade slowly away out of sight.
Drift alone, so lonely along until you falter to the ground.

Now only loving this one gets,
it pours onto itself.
I've become a cannibal,
these hands are the only pair here.
Urges of a cannibal, cravings for the kind of meat I need.

Pouring my own love, back out onto myself,
not enough remains to help my esteem.
Write and reach so much but no one wants me.

Funny, the entirety of my yesterdays,
Stand-alone under a street lamp.
Each with its own... for every good and bad,
hurt and loss, pain and guilt.
Come dear friend; come for connection and save me.

Come, come dear friend,
I'm just so tired of life... its all just too figured out,
We'll consume our way out; Pleasure and appetite await.

Remove these bricks, unpeel the cannibal,
Uncover this undiscovered love.
Run along the country hillside boulevard,
Retrieve the memories in street lamp light... one by one.
Come, won't you feast on me?
I want you, my love.
With the passion of a cannibal.

The Things the Hands of Change Can Never Touch

Wisp many particles,
molecules mixed with chemicals,
brings forth a flood.
Ocean of planets here!
Metaphors road journeyed
and laboured upon.
Collision gives you friction,
now can't we spontaneously combust?

Lingering presences in and out,
Thoughts and memories of lessons,
poor destiny...
Laboured relentlessly to toil
and succumbed to fate.

Bubbling water sizzles and steams,
chemicals transform the molecules
into vicious indescribable change
which comes with movement.

Here is the only door now
with freedom to the approaching step-gate.
What's out and able to be used?
To change this stubborn old mind
and stop all the movement and collision here.

For the Love of the Flower

Pushing up through the cement,
cracks run from edge to curb.
Beautiful flowers boasts
"Ha ha! I am resilient against your
fortress, strong enough to survive."

It flourishes over the course of the day,
collecting sunlight, water and punishment.
The migration of many trample it and
so it dies but leaves its roots.

Growing again it is trampled,
Twice in vain, twice to resolve.
Sunlight and rain not enough to save
the essence, energy of the flower.
Needs some care... needs some love.

Pick, shovel remove the surrounding,
suffocating walls in work.
Brings the sweat beading down.
"I'll save you dear flower!" I call to it
under concrete and footprints.

A Hand Through the Storm

Warm ceiling beams in a lot of light.
Smiles with eager eye's welcoming you in,
and flowing forth is claimed change.

Buried coins and quarters,
under garbage mixed with treasure.
Possibilities studied by its details
which the light offers to us with respect.

Lucks laugh comes in rigid and forceful.
We have a good single thing between us as
we now welcome in this wanted,
exhausted and changing love.

Now hold on, keep holding on,
to each other's hand through this storm of life.

Life

Living and loving,
laughing and crying.
Going through situations and learning what you may…
Staying true
and to care for simply asking
and doing what we can according as it comes.
Welcoming what sunrise colours bring
and the sunset colours and what they put to rest.
Now isn't that what life is?

Your Heart in Mine

I feel like I'm crying inside
but really I'm numb.
Everyone is a thief,
originality is long dead,
and definitely always loved.

Going back and reading what is written
in the book of our very lives will not change the winds
that blow the storms and rain our way.

I want to survive,
to make it and keep it!
Die with it,
for you my love are it.

So fill my sky with sunrises and sunsets,
taking on all new and old alike, one time!
Let your wind blow your rain
and grey rolling clouds my way.

Because the love flame that burns
inside of this sensitive and seasoned soul
is your heart in mine.

To Fly Away From Inside of Here

New things enter our lives,
by means of wind, word of mouth or karma.
Thoughts fill my head, each one with a face.

Change glides with the wind, a seagull soaring above rooftops.
Solid grey ceiling to this world,
envy sets in (but only for a moment).

To look down upon my surroundings,
the coming obstacles weep as I can so easily see both sides
and glide with the wind past them.
I could have hindsight before too late!

You assume these embers are of fear
but nothing inside of here shows that.
Journey along the paths knowing experience is the boss.

But just to know we could have knowledge for once.
I can tell you I feel something is tiring,
however I've been waiting for you to see that for yourself.
Wont you come to take a look inside of here,
oh questioning one?

New

Dark meadows and crying frustration.
Beautiful day when the clouds are scattered and the
colours of every type dance and spread across
these skies before my eyes.

Fear seeps in with total control,
no rest needed for the wicked.
Rapid mind and pounding, beating feet,
it would be nice to know all things could come to an end.

There are people living below me,
for which the embers of hate glow for.
Nothing needed to be done to the past;
It's been sealed but my gentle warm embrace knows it not.

Objects are moving and gears are turning,
I think my mind has been spewing out from the vault
of countless paintings that is my subconscious.
Feedback is all I want, it is all I need and options will be there.

Heavy darkness fills my head,
I fear I've really lost the way tonight,
In the darkness throughout this basement.
And yeah I killed the trudging man in that blizzard,
so my sleep could bring back the memories once more.
Figured out the conspiracy yes and yet still my heart remains
scared, hoping, full of faith and beating in the rhythm of this age old fear.

Pressure

Well I saw a person of the human kind
coming out through thick skin.
Intolerance caving in over reality.

Yes, lost beneath the high,
So our space cadet failed;
Walls stuck between.

Take it from the far dark hollows in the trees
and listen to the crushing aloneness.
Especially see the ringing.

Shuffled dirt, beading mind of thoughts
and pulsing temple in calculation.
Overlooking that every colour together is a rainbow;
Walks from mountains, deserts, prairies and forests-
Makes up the world and things we want.
Every colour mixed together is black;
Forgotten memories, decay and shadows.
We all come from many; not one.

Earth to Man to Earth

Slight breeze rustling through the leaves,
heavy solid expression upon all the faces.
I wish I could escape word and action and
the formulas that will, I am sure, come to let me
know the feeling of reality's touch again!

A crows looking down on me; craw! Craw!
I wonder what he's thinking (just like he is to me).
Perhaps its "Silly humans, always searching for
the perfect reaction you new-new world apes."

Down the sides of the passage ways here in town,
There's enough people around to make it feel lighter
than this, although. Thoughts and smiles and eyes and customs.

Do we ever really justify?
Caught between a rock and a hard place,
damned if we do and damned if we don't.
I won't elaborate on that entrapment of society, no not again.

Behold that is how we secure ourselves and our
freedoms away from it.
So through the forest I walk, with the dark shadows
filling in the underbrush far off all sides of the winding path.

Out to the ocean and down to the dock to the little rowboat.
Bouncing and bobbing with the waves.
Climbing over the edge and into it, I row from shore.
Out into the bay and up the river on the other side.

Taken to a lake and to the other side,
the base of the mountain stands before me and me it.
Straight into each other we stare for a long while and finally
we both hear within our own hearts as plain as words spoken
with soundwave ripples in the air,
"Still I have not been able to tame you!"

Self-Made Age of Symbolism

Grass swaying and bobbing in, out and all about.
Drifting clouds soar between me and the flashy
colour orb above the sky.

Drifting, sailing farther across and away,
its forever coming full circle again those clouds.
Bringing the rain and I'm thinking
"Saxophones and rain belong together."

But perhaps an old bridge still stands,
overgrown in the thickest part of the wood.
One that hasn't collapsed yet and remains
to hold the link between music and non-physical aspects of us humans.

Nothing within my soft, fleshy shell can stand as unrelenting,
as the statues on the hill symbolizing those who had died in the wars
defending belief and traditions and culture.

For our freedom and ability to move 360 degrees.
To piece things like this together without threat or worry.
We are all not so bad as blind rats or soulless, dead walking creatures.

But truly I believe we are what we make ourselves.
If not in the physical world, then in symbolism and metaphor;
close your lips all naysayers!
Doesn't principle stand for all things these days?

To Live

At times throughout my day things, thoughts and plans change,
delving in and searching low and only able to return by lifting my chin
and swimming to the sparkling water top of blanketed rippling white.

Snowy fields with race cars, later to lose their steering wheels to my boots.
Flaming steel model cars, broken in half and a lot of dinkies torn up and away too.
Sorrow and desires to twist exhibited by others to me,
were perhaps felt in the pains of those childhood J.I.Joes.
These things settle before my memory's eyes.
But this a life to live and to treasure, if not then why would we hold memories
and feel the emotions of life?

In later years from the torn and unrightful beginning,
there was tyranny and contempt mixing with shut-eye's
which coloured it all in black and cloudy memory colours.

No no… yeah your right, never has settled on a blended mixed colour yet.
Open streets and good health seem to be the desire of all.
Some journey to smell the grey rolling clouds (or coloured rocks, or strong juices)
and love the rain and lightning.
Snow or hail will come riding on its heels this next twelve or so hours.
Some seek the memory-blanking waves for smiles and loose-feeling joy,
for others its responsibility or recluse.
But we all have hearts and minds with which to write this book of life.

From when we experience years of toy filled youth,
to the lessons of good and bad.
We learned from our friends and elders up through adolescence.
To our adulthood where we continually (at a personalized rate) attempt to
finish the puzzle picture of our desired paths of life.

We must learn that the desire to live is in all of us.
For those who commit suicide, they are lost because they were battered.
For those who get up and fight, they still hold chance at happiness and peace.
But make no mistake, they both do what they do because
they have wanted or want to live.

Sombre Reflections

Alit in shadows as they dance and turn.
Mingling with their partners of their rhythmic pattern.
They steal the movement from my awaiting-to-smile lips,
Laid upon my face nothing but an opening for interpretation.

So side to side my head moves and twists,
to wist the casting light.
Searching to find the music box,
Each turn and shift of the line has these eyes hunting the answer
in wake of more memories at each sight.

Distance factual, there is the pavement upon the road from here to there.
Cast aside now and found in a pile; so much of what was once.
As more is placed upon the stack of albums to play there will be not a chance.

For clarity, for rest, for resolve.
So it all falls back down again.
This tower built of intensions of constructive desires.
Instead, in its place, we have the mysteries of what might have been
and of what now is.

Asking

We call while searching for the words,
ungrounding insects delight at the smell of our feet.
Feces' gathering in a mound behind us
and the minds of millions chattering.

The wind blows high and into the air,
anything that can be thought has been cast into this being of life.
We all try and we all care but no one can sum it all up.

The pavement leads across tree and brush,
pinching of insects and desire to kill.
We all have the paintbrushes of life in our own hands,
but some canvas' never hold the colours.

Mirrors held, considered jewels and priceless,
when across the room there stands foreign eyes.
Perhaps we're not so unlike those pinching insects,
which we desire to kill.

In those treeside bushes along this wretched, repeated
journeyed highway road of life they await.
But yet I'm still asking "What was it about the answer being
inside all of us!? It's funny how all faiths claim to have the one
golden rule… and yet that cannot be.
Nothing will ever be that relatable.
We're all unique and have the ability to change without end
and there's no exceptions to that… none!"

Slower, Simpler

Black hardened living replacer,
toxic offering furthering its list of things phased out.
Eyes and language of movement repel at an instant,
quicker along than the quicker form.

Abandon and treasure come as one
when back to our feets expeditions
it can be felt; once more.

Horses snorted and lower eye level
and sorrowingly nibble from
it's essence of life; its mending comfort.

Sad beasts and choices open,
more free than it was.
With that old hardened unthinking convenience.

Soft mane swishing from over shoulder looking.
Big easy eyes accept the affection of a
smooth palm from the affectionate
evolved ape who is appreciative;
both enjoy.

Something to Read

Buzzing in throughout the air
tiny electric waves... directions of sight.
Taking it all in and swelling to the brink,
everyone remembers everything,
so locked down tight!

Freedom is a paradox,
it is enigma.
It is blind ambition,
nothing short of impossible.

Greater, in today's world, is the focus
than the image.
Discredited and overrated
this realm is of birth and death.

Thousands elephants to hundreds of gallons,
Desperation well winning triumphantly over inspiration and passion.
Damnation of a generation,
collapse of identity.
Chameleons maybe the capitalists.
But it's those Reflectives that give birth.

Hurt, Loss and The Moving On

I can see heaven and the moon
are lost to your eyes.
I looking within those skies…
but all I see is rain.

Certainly I know you see
all these regrets in which I cannot forget.
I move to say them to you
but you stop me;
Saying tears are just sprinkles of the sands of time,
Oh wasted time.

So along on down this road
the silence brings the weight.
I cannot bring myself despite all this willingness
to find patience for this anymore.
So I guess these things are just better left unsaid,
they're better left unknown.
For what we thought we were,
is not what we are right now.

Now watch it all fall,
and falter to the ground.
Having a new mission fitted to our lives,
one that sends us searching for the sun.

Sudden

Paper to concentrate it.
Further and with observation.

Lingering through the fields
we usually run.
Standing afoot among the concave walls
we're standing within the desire.

Forcing and trying,
failing but trying.
Ring, ring go the calculation machines.
Purchased is a balance between
needs and inspiration.

Out of your skin, wash it off.
Flooding us through the drain.
I feel it to and yours and yours!
More than one person is what my eyes
see when observing myself.

Cleanly wiped from heaven,
standing in desires path (which it gave).
Talking and chatter of questions about
implications of myself.
Affecting pressure sweeps through.

Blank Canvas Crossroads

Down in the morning sun.
Drags with teeth and nail marks;
well it shatters everyone.

Now I willingly stand there,
piercing eyes and a tough hold sensation.
Determination gallops steady
like water or air.

Forever beneath shade or darkness.
For only within it can imagination be free.
A blank canvas chance,
can I find there a door that opens
out or in from here?

The Fire Was His Own

Efforts brimming hot and constant.
Images disturbed by this.
So to the hills journey is treading.

But still in the centre point,
smaller effects and improvements are produced.
Closer and faster his is built.
Subtlety and changes more in grasp,
each step landing moments of sweaty brow focus.

Searing pain tears you down
to a humble strength.
Winter air is cool on the face and jolting to the lungs.

A gaze to the sky with a deep cold breath.
Pause seized in the street there and then.
He stopped and so did the ripples in the water.
He could see the image now,
it was his face alit in flames!

Then and there he came to realize,
that the fire which he had been seeking,
that he had been longing to build for his own
(so that he may get his own dreams)
was his own all along.

Blind

Tapping, banging, ringing, flooding.
Standing in the pipeline,
unable to hear anything but
question and paranoia.

Straight ahead the light of day,
with a stream stretching into it
(From between the legs and far behind).
Darkness lays here clawing at the mind.

Eyes dart from light to dark.
Tomorrow seems so far away,
yet here we are in yesterdays.

Falling out of our skin comes the
sweat, the strain, desire… the regret.
Does a price always come forcefully
on to us or do we to it?

Emotions, sensations.
To experience and to put to life
our many types of thoughts and such.
Can we really say a dollar figure when we
do not see what we cost ourselves?

Speed and Fear

Flowing through time fast.
Choice lingers out of reach within our sight.
Chance is bitter and dripping with rivalry,
decorated in grudge.

Distinguish your desire,
from the rest which is moved by you.
Tears and true pain.
Under your power that enforces work upon me.

And in your stomach grinds the eternal suspicion.
Can there be time I ask to halt, wait and prepare?
For what will there be done when choice wins?
Kills chance and takes all for itself and halts
this forward momentum by declaring:
Onto each.....THEIR OWN!

Keep Away

Keep away,
Breeze through the trees,
Song whispers, whistles of the leaves,
Oh keep away.

Rain trickling down the window,
Pain just a game to you.
Reality grinds in now, still ever
deeper and what can be done?

Lonely sidewalks,
Aching desire for the warmth of love.
The hot throbbing of the back of my head (strain),
Oh just keep away.

Don't disturb it alive,
Keep this washing shield of numb!
I'm damn happy you can read me,
nothing but want of distance.

Afraid of the hurt to come,
Still coming onto me though
because of this self-imposed recluse…
No, but love is not forever anyway
just desire of it.
So forget and keep away.

Burst of Life

When the air holds heavy,
Blowing against my face,
I am left cold bitten and weather etched.

Overhead cloud cover locks all sky
and colour out tight.
Flowers lay there withered,
trees losing their instruments.

Companionship driven off at the
speed of the cold biting wind.
Nothing but paw and footprints left.
All empty, withered, slowly rotting river valley.

Thoughts crossing, crashing.
Only myself to see and feel and to talk.
Hot and anguished anger at me, at them and a
ringing, banging silence spreads across; no sense found.

Upon my hands and knees
I felt it then in my search for life.
The warmth and energy of it.
Up into my head from my chest,
shooting me up into the tree`s.
Spying, hearing and spotting you,
a coloured glimpse of what I have been searching for.

Down from the sky,
a hole in the clouds let in the light.
Bringing back to life my valley.

And the green to trees,
once again ringing aloud their calming melody,
The aroma of flowers enticing my nose
and the animals back to their nests and forging grounds.

All upon and around me,
and a beautiful explosion of force,

you came into my valley,
tore away the death clouds and coloured in all the dying.
Filling my heart continually with a warm,
burning and soothing special feeling.
It's running so deep,
as we do together down into this place of life.

Discontent

Just spill like the alcohol over my lips,
Words spewing forth like the acid reflux I induce upon myself.
This afternoon on the corner of the rooftops to my apartment building,
I saw a raven with the sunset lighting up the sky behind it.

The streets are a long-gone place that I have left far behind.
But for this I am happy for they are too lonely for me to bare any longer
(My youth's near entirety was of only them).
Also to mention, sky gazing is a passing-away comfort now.

A world where we may cross boundaries and openly speak our mind,
but will always face stern adversity for doing so- always a battle.
Many people believe (which includes me more than half the time)
that it will certainly also come from ourselves.

Still yet we rise to another day, searching for a way.
Trying to right all our wrongs we are eagerly anticipating recognition
for our struggles (and our intentions).

Trouble is; when I toss bread out to those ravens so they're hopping and
wing-fluttering for the pieces may take me away, I see conflict among them.
It's not an ugly thing, but a beautiful thing.
Their desire and strength to survive,
their willingness to fight!
It unsettles me though.

Lessons of Love

Slow, persistent pushing against myself,
Oh certainly the clanging links of change showed no weak link.
Ringing and voices in my head met, by me, with an abundance of tart;
Hysteria boiled up inside upon realizing I could not rid myself of that chain
(With its anchor firmly embedded; half in my dreams, half in my heart).

Could I prize myself from being so deaf upon these ears?
Throughout the first half extrication of it would not walk through my door,
But merely flash before my eyes within the distant figures I physically and eagerly
shook hands with.
Each, obviously, a representation:
Roots were but a duty to transcend and so was friendship, really.
The anchor, tore into both as it was so no wonder I could not find strength to
release!
So virulent seemed my dream to my heart;
Dissolution crept in once I came to understand what they were to each other.

I learned that's what happens when the sail hands hold when there's fierce wind;
something somewhere breaks.
Disrespect of the wind yields only perpetual hardships; come now, how else would
those flags of yours be flying!?
Against each other those changing links tore, broke and clattered away, taking with
it wood and railing.
This is what happens when a team has different horizons marked and compassed
upon the map.

Change, wise and unyielding, walked with a slow clunk, clunk, clunk into the room
and set it all too sombre.
Sitting in my drifting, damaged vessel I watched the sky sail the clouds on by.
Closed eyes and prayers with a whole lot of spite against the damage held me
through.
Repair was made in a dramatic and most honestly-heartfelt manner;
Never again, I swore, to push against myself; this I would never do!

Up to the dock I had marked and compassed,
I walked across the planks to the fields of fruit yielding labour;
My dream of a garden where there would be time for growing, nurturing and feast.
Dirty nails, aching back and a freedom I couldn't seem to immediately place.

244

In either loneliness or control, all I knew was that I could not grow the whole garden alone.

After sometime, and some vegetation had grown from my labours,
The finest maiden walked along my fence answered my request
and joined me in the garden.
A glimmer in my eyes she said showed her something of which
she'd been longing for.
The experience of pushing against oneself and the lesson;
When you sail for your dreams while your teammate sails for theirs
and yet you share the same vessel and refuse to accept this,
You will eventually be torn apart with damage left.
So choose, accept and never push against yourself.
What we saw... we shared; from it was a resolve to never repeat.
She had been dreaming of building the same garden as I!

Now, under the colours of sky and sun we work together,
Merrily aiding and letting be each other as is needed.
Teaching and feeding each other the fruits of our labour,
Truly now our freedom is one of peace and promise.
Being fully prized from deafness finally,
I realize from where the ringing and voices were coming;
They were a warning!
It was the groan of the wood under the pressure; the knocking of the chain before breaking.

North for the Unified

Most places have ground.
For gardens, for graves.
The entirety of all they have is situated
where they pick to lay it;
Nothing is easily pieced together.
All must labour around the rock here.

Standing beneath the setting sun for hours,
Before the fading light.
A constant, balanced battle;
Always slowly creeping for the darkness
escorting down its subtle, absolute impact.
Laid to rest each night; the day.

Careful observation amongst the flowers,
Will reveal handles, hinges and straps.
Burying away struggles underneath the ever illusive scented colour.
Some even with poles and high flying flags beside them.
The ground and rocks aren't enough to fly many questionable banners.

Clangs ring out loudly from the rattling of fallen
poles with their banners and flags.
The solo man painted in resentment as he possesses
so much but has not!

All laugh at cynicism since it is known
that to plant a garden here there must be a unity.
A joining of skills and hands.
To move some rock to pour some concrete,
To lay soil and hold the pole high to fly our banner!
There is no soil here in which to bury,
We must join hands to hold up the pole.
Your banners and flags must symbolize unity here dear newcomer.

So welcome North, isolated however never alone where
all flags and banners are held up by more than one pair of hands.

Fragile Light

Reaching off into the light.
Covered with jolts and dry mouth paste;
At the other end lays that curse.
Instead of question there is certainty about it.

Treading slowly along the length.
Once more I can begin to feel it.
One by one fall away every sight and
unsettling feeling as closer comes the light.

Limbo is a state with wide country but small roads.
Between all I remember, and most times when I don't,
And what there really is,
Lays the hot, burning vulnerability.

Perhaps it's due to loss of a
world where the next is not known.
Or rather, fear of being alone in the waking moment.
Looking back is that road leading back off into the darkness.

Dreaming in the Rainy Boulevard

Sometimes I have difficulty trudging through the day.
Seems my dreams and desires
are too hot and are slowly burning it all away.
Rain pattering upon cobblestones,
A viper leaps up against the shop window.
Spouts pour out many dreams which float from our heads;
Dashed in their effort to reach heaven.

Your always standing inside my mind; right in front of me.
So transparent that I can't clearly make out what there is to see.
Amongst the grass you may find the mud indentations of that man's boots,
during the storm he was trudging something heavy.

Now I'll just watch the physical things around me for a while
to put my mind at ease.
Watching the golden, white rain through the street lights
or perhaps I'll admire the cars and the wiper blades,
as they tear through the wall of dream thievery.

It was here for a while, but after a time it seemed to be someplace else!
And now I suppose the optimal response in life is to walk my chosen road,
Stand behind my chosen stand.

But still, as I walk through my life; journeying through the many sites I see,
It has grown tiresome standing here so long.... I think I might finally open my eyes.

Freedom and Father Time

In all of the places I have been and of all the things I have learned and really, the basis of my work and the general theme of "This Quest For That Final Horizon" is this:

With each passing day, father time steals from me a small portion of the wondrous mystery of life and leaves behind a piece of the puzzle that is life. Every day I'm learning something new but with that newly learned thing, I am losing a piece of my inner child. So I pick myself up and run so far and fast without relent or surrender. Eyeing the finish line; always on the horizon. Forever is that freedom on the horizon.

So maybe I'm not meant to reach it. Maybe it's unreachable so that I can have something to work towards, to keep running to, to have a purpose......... So here we have it. Freedom and Father Time work together.

www.ingramcontent.com/pod-product-compliance
Lightning Source LLC
LaVergne TN
LVHW011345080426
835511LV00005B/137